ON THE DIVINE LITURGY

ORTHODOX HOMILIES

VOLUME ONE

THE MOST REVEREND METROPOLITAN
AUGOUSTINOS N. KANTIOTES

Augoustinos N. Kantiotes
Bishop of Florina, Greece

ON THE
DIVINE LITURGY

ORTHODOX HOMILIES

VOLUME ONE

Translated and Foreworded
by
Asterios Gerostergios

Institute for Byzantine and Modern Greek Studies
115 Gilbert Road
Belmont, Massachusetts 02178

On the Divine Liturgy, Orthodox Homilies, originally appeared in Greek under the title, Εἰς τὴν Θείαν Λειτουργίαν, Πρακτικαὶ Ὁμιλίαι, published by the Orthodox Missionary Brotherhood, "Ὁ Σταυρός" ("The Cross"), Athens, 1977. The author dedicated this first volume to "those who enter the Holy House for the Divine Liturgy 'with faith, reverence, and fear of God.' " We dedicate this translation to the author himself on the occasion of his fiftieth anniversary as a clergyman-preacher of the Orthodox Church, fondly expressing our gratitude for his kind permission and encouragement toward the translation and publication of this work.

All rights reserved.
Copyright © 1986, by Asterios Gerostergios
Published by THE INSTITUTE FOR BYZANTINE
AND MODERN GREEK STUDIES, INC.
115 Gilbert Road, Belmont, Massachusetts 02178, U.S.A.
Library of Congress Catalog card Number: 85-81949
Printed in the United States of America

Complete set ISBN 0-914744-71-2
This volume ISBN 0-914744-72-0

TRANSLATOR'S FOREWORD

Preaching the divine word, be it spoken or written, is a most difficult undertaking. Its purpose is the spiritual cultivation of God's people, to help them know Christ the Savior, believe in Him, and live in accord with the Gospel precepts.

The servant of the divine word should be adorned with the Christian virtues, and have a good Christian reputation, for only in this way can his words be powerful, convincing, effective.

In our own times, one such brilliant ecclesiastical figure, adorned with such qualities is the Most Reverend Bishop of Florina, Greece, Augoustinos N. Kantiotes. This distinguished churchman is known for his magnificently successful work in the Church of Greece, and is universally recognized for his efforts on behalf of the Orthodox Church, where he excels in the spoken and written word. His writings are truly astonishing. His numerous books, totaling thousands of pages, as well as his articles in periodicals and newspapers, have spiritually nourished the Greek people for decades, and will continue to do so. Bishop Augoustinos is a many – talented and exceptional contemporary personality, a treasure of the Church of Greece, and of Orthodoxy as a whole.

Together with so many other Christians, we have had the opportunity of being nourished by the preaching of this excellent man, and are therefore humbly and thankfully dedicating the present translation of his sermons to him, on the occasion this very learned and respected Hierarch's fiftieth anniversary as a cleric – preacher of the Church. "Your own of your own we offer you," beloved, most reverend Father, Teacher and blessed Hierarch!

We decided to give our English-speaking Orthodox people these sermons of the Bishop of Florina, believing they will fill a void, for there are no such sermons in the English language. Moreover, these unique sermons offer to Christian people purely Orthodox spiritual food. As a skillful and noble servant of the divine word, the author introduces the reader to the lofty meaning of the Divine Liturgy. Using many examples and images from contemporary life as well as from history, he makes the Liturgy accessible and understandable, and leads the reader to feel ardent love for Christ and His Orthodox Church.

The present volume, containing the interpretation of the first part of the Divine Liturgy, called the Liturgy of the Catechumens, will be followed by a second one, having an interpretation of the remainder of the Divine Liturgy, the Liturgy of the Faithful.

We believe, along with the distinguished author-hierarch, that the genuine Orthodox food offered here to clergy and laity will have a warm reception, and will fulfill its purpose: the rekindling of love for the Divine Liturgy and Orthodox worship in general, and of the aspiration to live in accordance with the precepts of Christ.

The translation and publication was a difficult and costly endeavor. But with God's grace it has been achieved. Among those who worked with me to publish this work were our friends Steve and Anna Yannakopoulos, Savvas Zembilas, and George K. Duvall who read the first draft of my translation and made numerous corrections and suggestions for improving it; and Constatine Cavarnos and Stanley Butler, who helped me prepare the text for publication. May the Lord remember their valuable contributions.

Finally, I would like to thank Stephen and Catherine Pappas for their generous financial assistance. May the Lord return their generosity in heavenly blessings.

ASTERIOS GEROSTERGIOS

PREFACE

The church is the center of the liturgical life for Orthodox Christians. Inside the church, the faithful live and receive the Grace of the Holy Mysteries. The greatest opportunity for receiving Divine Grace is the celebration of the Divine Liturgy.

The Divine Liturgy is not merely a gathering of the faithful. It is the union of the faithful with each other. It is the union of the Church Militant here on earth with the Church Triumphant in heaven. Most of all, it is the union of the faithful with Christ. In the Divine Liturgy, the faithful travel together through all of the stages of Christ's life on earth. Together with the shepherds, they visit the manger of Bethlehem. Together with the simple people of Galilee, they observe the entry of Christ into public life. Together with the multitude which "was astonished at His teaching," they listen to Christ's Gospel, which is Wisdom. Together with a few select souls, they travel with Christ as He climbs up Golgotha to His Passion and are "crucified with" Christ. Together with the Myrrh-bearing women, they experience the joy of the Resurrection. Every stage of the life of Christ is repeated in the Divine Liturgy.

God's gift in the Divine Liturgy is priceless. The gift of being able to attend is priceless. Even more priceless is the gift of being able to become a partaker of the Divine Supper, sharing the same body and blood with Christ.

Unfortunately, only a few Christians understand the great gift of the Divine Liturgy. Most are totally indifferent and do not regularly attend the Divine Liturgy; or else they regularly attend the Divine Liturgy, but nevertheless remain cold observers of the events in the church, passive recipients of what is heard in the Divine Liturgy, unmoved spectators of the divine Drama. They listen without interest to what is said and chanted. They gaze upon the Holy Chalice and Paten, but remain unmoved.

There are many reasons why those who attend the Divine Liturgy lack zeal. One of these is ignorance. Many people do not know what is said and what happens during the Divine Liturgy. The language seems unintelligible to them, the meaning incomprehensible, the proceedings enigmatic.

Accordingly, there is need for enlightenment. In the Divine Liturgy lie hidden treasures which are completely unknown to many people. It contains a hidden heavenly wealth. Many people who are ignorant of this wealth live in the poverty of material things. There is need for this wealth to become known to many people. All can enjoy this wealth.

The short sermons in this book are an effort to enable people who are uninformed to know and enjoy the riches of the Divine Liturgy. The bishop of Florina, the leader of our Brotherhood, Father Augoustinos, has been working for the past two years on themes pertaining to the church and the Divine Liturgy in a series of short sermons, which are published in the pamphlet *Kyriake*, "Sunday," distributed free each Sunday in the churches of his Diocese. The sermons of 1975 were devoted to the church building, to its various parts, as well as to the various services which take place inside it. They were published in a book entitled *The Orthodox Church*. The sermons of 1976 were devoted to the Divine Liturgy, especially to the first part, the Liturgy of the Catechumens. These are published in the present book, *ON THE DIVINE LITURGY*. With God's help, there will be a third series of sermons, devoted to the second part of the Divine Liturgy, the Liturgy of the Faithful.

The sermons published are not theological discussions of the Divine Liturgy. They are practical sermons about the chief points in the Liturgy of the Catechumens. The Gospel dominates this part, while the Holy Chalice dominates the second part. Through the Gospel, through catechism and through preaching, the Christian is introduced to the mystery of the Divine Liturgy.

May these practical homilies contribute to the awakening of interest in understanding and appreciating the Divine Liturgy, so that Christians might become conscious partakers of the liturgical wealth of our Church.

Athens, November 21, 1976
Feast of the Presentation of the All-Holy Virgin Mary in the Temple.
Orthodox Missionary Brotherhood of *Ho Stavros* ("The Cross")

CONTENTS

BEFORE THE
DIVINE LITURGY

"THE SHADOW"

With the help of our Lord, my brothers and sisters, let us begin a new series of practical homilies. Let us interpret the Divine Liturgy.

The Divine Liturgy opens with : "Blessed be the Kingdom of the Father, and of the Son, and of the Holy Spirit." It closes with the words: "Through the prayer of the Holy Fathers . . .." Then the priest distributes the consecrated bread to all who have come together to worship.

The Divine Liturgy is a mystery: it is the mystery of mysteries. If the Lord enlightens our minds and enflames our hearts, so that we can hear and participate in this mystery, then we cannot remain cold and indifferent to it. Instead, a deeply felt gratitude towards our great benefactor, the Triune God, will reign in our hearts.

In the early days of the Church, the Christians, moved by faith, would attend the Liturgy with deep feeling, their eyes filled with tears and their hearts with true prayers. Let us pray that we may see the return of those days, and that the Liturgy may again be attended with the seriousness due to the holy. It is towards this end that we direct our interpretation of the Liturgy.

Many theologians and scholars of our Church have written wise books which discuss each detail of the Liturgy, and Christians can take refuge from their doubts in these great works. Our homilies, however, are not intended for the scholars but for the simplest among us. To those Christians who thirst to learn about the Liturgy, these homilies are like a glass of water offered from the inexhaustible spring of our holy religion.

Before we begin the interpretation of the Divine Liturgy, we should say a few words about its purpose, so that everyone, even the least educated, can have an idea about it from the very outset.

Let us begin far back in time, in the early years of the Old Testament. Many things that happened in those days were like hints, previews of events to come in the New Testament. Christ can be seen in the Old Testament, though not always clearly. He is dimly visible, like the face of a man reflected on the water's surface. In the New Testament, He appears not as a shadow but clearly as the true Christ, the Son of God, Who came to save the world.

You have heard of how the Hebrews, God's chosen people, lived as slaves under the tyrannical rule of the king of Egypt, the Pharoah. For more than four hundred years they were enslaved, before God took pity on them and moved to free them. He sent Moses to be their liberator. Moses appeared before Pharoah and demanded, in the name of God, that the Hebrews be released. But Pharoah would not hear of it. And so God, to punish Pharoah, and to induce him to let His people go, sent plagues. But Pharoah, even after nine terrible plagues, was not moved.

At last God, sent the tenth and most terrible plague. He sent an angel of death by night to kill all the first-born males of Egypt, from the princes of the palace to the children of the poorest huts. But before He let loose this frightful punishment, God told Moses to warn His

people of what was to happen. Moses directed every
Hebrew family to kill a lamb and to mark their door-
posts with its blood. This would be a sign to the angel
of death to pass over their homes that night. They were
to roast the lamb; to eat it with care, so as not to break
even one of its bones; to eat it with bitter herbs and
unleavened bread; and to eat it quickly at dawn, ready
for departure.

And indeed, what God said would happen, *did*
happen. An angel of the Lord came that night and killed
the first-born sons of the Egyptians. He spared only those
families that had marked their doors with the blood of
the lamb. So great was the calamity that hit the Egyptian households that, on the same night, Pharoah sum-
moned Moses and told him: "You and your people are
free to leave this hour and to return to your homeland"
(Exod. Chapters 11-12).

God called on the Hebrews to celebrate this event
as their greatest and most important holy day. This feast
day was called Passover, because on that day God's
people passed over from slavery to freedom.

Three thousand five hundred years have passed
since that first Passover, and it remains today the greatest
and most seriously observed holy day of the Hebrews.
It is celebrated by the Jews of today almost the same
as it was by their forefathers in Egypt. Passover falls
regularly on the 14th of Nisan, which coincides with our
April. Every Jewish household kills a lamb, roasts it on
a spit and eats it with bitter herbs and unleavened bread.
The family seated around the table does not merely eat
a special meal; they perform a religious ceremony. The
head of the family opens the ceremony by raising a glass
and praising God for all the good things He has done

for His people. The family then joins him in singing hymns. The youngest child asks why they eat unleavened bread and bitter herbs, and the eldest male replies with the story of the first Passover. And so the Jews continue to carry out God's commandment that the Passover be observed and celebrated by every generation (Exod. 12:14).

But this holy day of Passover that the Jews celebrate is only a shadow of the actual Passover, that which we Christians celebrate. For what does the sheep killed by the Jews signify? It signifies our Lord Jesus Christ. Christ, as proclaimed by John the Baptist, is the Lamb of God who takes the sins of the world. The blood of the lamb saved the Hebrews from frightful catastrophe; the blood of Christ, who like a lamb was sacrificed on Golgotha, saves every believing soul from the eternal destruction. This is proof that the lamb of the Hebrews points to our Lord Jesus Christ: the Hebrews were ordered not to break any bones when eating the lamb. "A bone of it ye shall not break" (Exod. 12:10). This seems a strange command. But it is made clear by what happened to Christ on Good Friday: when Pilate's soldiers received orders to take down the bodies of the crucified Christ and of the two thieves, they broke the legs of the living thieves, but they did not break Christ's legs, for He was already dead. And so the prophecy was fulfilled::"No bone of his shall be broken" (St. John 19:36).

"THE REALITY"

The Jews, as we have said in the last homily, have as their greatest holy day the Passover. But this Passover was only a shadow of the true Passover, the true Passover of Christ. Christ became man and offered Himself as sacrifice so that the promise of the Hebrew Passover would be fulfilled. Now that Christ has come in the flesh, we need no longer pay homage to His shadow.

Christ is the true Passover. That this is so can be seen not only by what we said last week, but also by what Christ said and did on the night of Holy Thursday. On that night, He celebrated what we Orthodox Christians know as the Mystical Supper. This homily is about the Mystical Supper.

On the day before the Hebrews were to celebrate their own Passover, the Apostles, at Christ's bidding, sought out and found a suitable room in a friendly house in Jerusalem, and in that room, on the night of Great ("Holy") Thursday, Christ celebrated His own Passover, the true and eternal Passover. It was certainly not Christ's celebration of the Hebrew feast, for the Hebrews celebrated their Passover sitting upright, whereas Christ and His disciples reclined on cushions, leaning on their left elbows and taking food with their right hands. More importantly, if Christ had celebrated the Hebrew Passover one day before the fixed day, then that would have been an obvious violation of God's own command, and

Judas, who was present, would certainly have reported this violation to Christ's enemies, who would in turn have used this serious accusation to enflame the crowds against Christ. But it was indeed His own Passover, the Christian Passover, that Christ celebrated that night of Great Thursday. How did He perform it?

We are told by the Evangelist Matthew: after they had sat at the table and eaten, Christ took bread in His holy hands, gave thanks to His heavenly Father, blessed the bread, broke it, and gave a piece to each disciple, saying: "Take, eat. This is my body." He then took the cup full of wine and gave it to His disciples, saying: "Drink this, all of you. This is my blood of the New Covenant, which is shed for many so that sins may be forgiven. I tell you I shall not drink again of this fruit of the vine until the day when I drink it new with you in my Father's Kingdom" (Matt. 26:26-29).

These are words of great importance. Their meaning is clear and they do not allow for misinterpretation. But still various heretics have tried to give another meaning to these words of Christ's, because their small minds have not been able to comprehend that the bread which Christ blessed became His own true body, and the wine His own true blood. Because I cannot understand something, must I deny it and reject it? If we were to begin this way, we would not be able to stop. Because not just one thing, but many things, many thousands of things, which we see and feel we would have to deny, for we cannot explain them.

Should I cite some examples? Consider the grapevine. This has roots. The roots absorb water and various other substances from the soil. These become sap, which, after having been pressed out of the grapes, becomes wine. Ask, if you will, an agriculturist to explain how this takes place; he will not be able to answer you. Some mystery is buried here which scientists cannot uncover. And yet, even though we cannot understand this process, we happily accept the wine and drink it. We don't say: "I cannot explain it, so I refuse to drink it!"

Another example. Men eat bread. This bread, together with the other foods that we eat, through the mysterious chemistry of the human organism, becomes blood. The blood circulates and nourishes the entire organism, and it in turn becomes nerves, nails, bones, flesh. How do these changes take place? A mystery! And yet who can deny it, simply because he cannot explain it? We cannot explain how the food the mother eats becomes blood and the blood milk. Isn't this a mystery?

Another example? There are certain rare stones called diamonds. They are worth millions. Diamonds were once carbon, carbon buried deep in the earth, which changed and became diamonds. How? A mystery!

As if these were the only mysteries! Mysteries abound in our wonderful world. Let the proud man who does not want to believe in Christ's words first explain the mysteries in front of his eyes before questioning the logic of the Mystery of mysteries, the Holy Communion.

The communion that the disciples received at the Lord's Supper is the same that we the faithful continue to receive today. We receive the body and the blood of Christ. Christ is an inexhaustible fountain from which believers everywhere, and always, drink and are spiritually nourished. Consider the sun, which every day sends countless millions of rays to the earth, and so in some way becomes countless millions of pieces, and yet remains one inexhaustible sun. The Christ we receive in Holy Communion is like the sun. A Mystery!

Christ Himself gave us an image of the greatest miracles, Holy Communion, in another miracle performed earlier in His ministry. One day a great crowd followed Christ into the desert to hear Him speak. The day wore on, and the sun was about to set, and the crowd had to be fed. But where would the disciples find food for so many people? It would take thousands of loaves to satisfy the crowd, and the disciples had only five loaves and two fish. And so Christ performed His miracle. He took the loaves and fish, blessed them, and then began to break them and distribute the pieces to the crowd. Piece after piece He broke from each loaf, but the bread did not run out. It multiplied continuously.

This was the miracle performed in the desert. From this we get an idea of what happens in Holy Communion. The bread and the wine, which Christ blessed at the Lord's Supper and which continues to be blessed and made holy through the intercessions of the priest, in some miraculous way increases and multiplies on the altar. From this the generations of Christians will partake until the end of time. They all receive the body and blood of Christ "for the forgiveness of sins and life everlasting."

This is the Christian Passover here on earth. But there will be another Passover, infinitely superior, the Passover to the other life, which will be earned by those who are worthy in this life to partake of the body and blood of Christ.

"Great art Thou, O Lord, and wondrous art Thy works, and no word will suffice to hymn Thy wonders!"

THE OFFERTORY

For the celebration of the Divine Liturgy, we need, besides the holy vessels, three things: bread, wine, and water. By these we show that our souls need spiritual nourishment. The heavenly food that our souls need is even more satisfying than the manna which sustained the Hebrews during their forty years in the desert. The word of God is our spiritual bread, our heavenly manna. The true bread that came down from heaven so that souls may be fed is Christ Himself. It is His precious body and blood which is offered to the faithful through the mystery of the Divine Eucharist. This the Lord emphatically declared:

"Verily, verily, I say unto you, Except ye eat the flesh of the Son of man, and drink his blood, ye have no life in you. Whoso eateth my flesh, and drinketh my blood, hath eternal life; and I will raise him up at the last day" (John 6:53-54).

Christ used bread to celebrate the Mystery of the Divine Eucharist. Before wheat becomes bread, it goes through many stages. It grows from seed to stalk to ear to grain. Think of the care, the labor, the pain that goes into making a loaf of bread! The tractor plows the earth: the farmer sows the seeds; the seed soaks up water, soil, and sun, and matures; the harvesters swing the heavy sickle for days, and then bow down low to collect the stalks into bundles; the stalks are beaten on the threshing floor; the grain is ground, sifted, kneaded into dough, and finally baked in the oven. All this must be done with love and patience.

Christ takes the bread, blesses it, and changes it into His precious body. He likewise blesses the wine and makes it His blood. Christ is completely present in every crumb of the blessed bread and in every drop of the sanctified wine.

Without bread, wine, and water, the Divine Eucharist cannot be offered.

The faithful Christians bring the bread and wine to the Church, for the celebration of the Divine Liturgy. The priest should not accept gifts for the celebration of the Divine Liturgy from people who have sinned publicly and remain unrepentant. The gifts must come from Christians who have confessed and are struggling to live a Christian life. The priest receives their gifts and prepares for the Divine Liturgy in a short service called the Offertory, or Proskomide.

The Offertory (Proskomide) takes place as follows:

1. The priest stands before the Beautiful Gate of the Iconostasion and strengthens himself with a series of prayers, beginning with: "Lord, have mercy on me, a sinner." Then, reciting certain troparia (hymns), he venerates and kisses in succession the Holy Icons of Christ, the All-Holy Virgin Mary, St. John the Forerunner, and the Patron Saint of the Church. He ends with a special prayer, in which he beseeches the Lord to enable him to celebrate the Divine Liturgy blamelessly, without accusation by his conscience for any serious offense.

2. He then enters the Holy Sanctuary, where he makes three acts of reverence before the Holy Altar and kisses both the Book of the Gospel and the Altar, saying again: "Lord have mercy upon me, a sinner." He then puts on his vestments, blessing and kissing each one of them

and reciting verses from Scripture that stress the virtues with which the priest should be adorned. When the priest stands before the Holy Altar, says St. Chrysostom, he should shine brighter than the sun by his possession of many virtues.

3. After vesting himself, the priest goes to the wash-stand and washes his hands, saying: "I will wash my hands among the innocents, and so will I go around Thy Altar . . . ."

4. As the service of the Matins (Orthros) continues, the priest moves on to the Holy Credence. The Credence is a niche in the wall to the left of the Holy Altar. This niche represents the holy cave in which the Saviour of the world was born under the poorest conditions. And so, as we prepare to offer the Divine Liturgy, we call to mind the birth of our Holy Religion. It was born in a cave. There follows the baptism in the Jordan River, the temptations in the desert, the public ministry of Christ, His crucifixion, resurrection, and finally the ascension. Christ's whole life, from cave to clouds, is represented in the Divine Liturgy. The faithful Christian lives the mystery of the incarnation and participates in Holy Communion. The priest sings this hymn as he stands before the Holy Credence: "O Bethlehem, be ready. Eden has been opened to everyone."

5. The priest then takes one of the loaves of oblation or *prosphora* offered by the faithful. The *prosphoron* symbolizes the Mother of God, for it was by way of her body that Christ was born in the flesh. Holding the loaf in his left hand and the lance in his right, and touching the lance to the seal stamped on the *prosphoron*, the priest elevates them both to the level of his head, saying: "Thou hast redeemed us from the curse of the law by Thy precious Blood . . . ." Then he makes the sign of the Cross

over the Credence with the loaf and the lance, reciting: "Blessed is our God, always, now and forever and from all ages." Then he makes the sign of the cross three times over the seal of the *prosphoron,* saying each time: "In remembrance of our Lord and God and Saviour Jesus Christ." He then thrusts the lance into the right side of the central square of the seal, then into the left, then above, then below, reciting with each thrust the corresponding prophecy of Isaiah: "He was led as the sheep to the slaughter." "And as a lamb before his shearer is dumb, so he opens not His mouth." "In His humiliation justice was denied Him." "Who shall declare His generation?" Then he inserts the lance beneath the seal and lifts up the cubic portion of the bread, the "Amnos" or "Lamb," on which are stamped the letters IC-XC NIKA, "Jesus Christ Conquers." This he places on the Holy Paten, pierces it crosswise with the lance, reciting verses from the Bible which call to mind Christ's crucifixion. The priest then pours wine and water into the Holy Chalice, covers it, and puts it aside.

6. Next, he cuts from the *prosphoron* a triangular piece in honor of the Blessed Virgin Mary, and this is placed at the right side of the Lamb. Then three rows of three small pieces each are cut on the other side of the Lamb in honour of the apostles, martyrs, and other saints. In front of the Lamb, two rows of smaller pieces are arranged in memory of the living and the dead for whom the Liturgy will be celebrated. The priest then puts the asterisk, symbolizing the star of Bethlehem, on the Paten, and covers with veils both the Paten and the Chalice. He censes the Covered Holy Gifts three times, and finally chants the beautiful closing prayer of the offertory service.

CHRIST THE MERCIFUL

I

THE GREAT
SUPPLICATION

THE BEGINNING OF THE DIVINE LITURGY

"Blessed be the Kingdom of the Father, and of the Son, and of the Holy Spirit, now and forever, and for all ages to all ages."

The Divine Liturgy, my dear brethren, is the most important service of our Holy Church. It is miraculous, a masterpiece of the Spirit. It is like a magnificent building, erected by the wisest architects according to an inspired plan. Many people admire great buildings of the past and of the present. They come from all over the world to pay homage to the Parthenon, built atop the Acropolis by our ancestors, as a monument of Greek art and wisdom. But the Orthodox Christians are privileged to know the most magnificent spiritual monument of all: our Divine Liturgy! In the Liturgy, as in an architectural work, everything has its proper place. The architects of the Liturgy used, instead of stones, precious prayers and concepts. They mined their materials from the Old and the New Testaments, arranged and connected them to achieve an architectural harmony. The hearts and minds of all those who enter this structure are lifted up to the heavens, where Christ mediates on behalf of sinners forever. Christ, then, is the cornerstone, the cement, the center, and the crown of this mystical monument, the Divine Liturgy.

He who has good intentions, a mystical ear to hear, and a mystical eye to see, is dazzled by the spiritual beauty of the Divine Liturgy. When men who had been converted by missionaries from the darkness of idolatry to the light of Christianity attended the Divine Liturgy for the first time, they could not find words to express their wonder.

If the Divine Liturgy is celebrated and attended with faith, it is enough to demonstrate that ours is the true religion. In no other religion in this world, in no religious service of the non-Christian world, is there the grandeur which shines in our Divine Liturgy. How unfortunate, then, for those of us who were born into the Orthodox Church and who are unaware of the Divine Liturgy's value! How many of us think it is a burden to attend the Liturgy, and, all the while we are there, wait anxiously for it to end. Such people are like those who are insensitive to a musical symphony conducted by a brilliant maestro. Instead, they are excited by cheap bouzoukis, by shameful songs, by conversations so disgusting as to make any decent man sick to his stomach. The Lord speaks of such people as pigs, who love their corruption as pigs love mud, and who therefore don't know what to do with diamonds (Matt. 7:6). O Lord, save us from such insensitivity and callousness!

The opening lines of the Divine Liturgy are the majestic entrance through which we come into this great spiritual work. The priest begins by proclaiming: "Blessed be the Kingdom of the Father, and of the Son, and of the Holy Spirit, now and forever and from all ages to all ages. Amen." What is the meaning of these words, which we hear every time we go to church? Let us take care, my brethren, for if we hear these words without our minds comprehending the divine meanings they contain, we will not experience deep emotions. We will enter and leave the church unmoved, with no substantial benefit.

"Blessed be the Kingdom." We praise, bless and glorify with all our strength; we express our love and admiration for the Kingdom. Whose kingdom is it? It does not belong to this or that worldly ruler, who lives today and dies tomorrow, but to God. Yes, it is the kingdom of God! God reigns and governs over His kingdom. But what is His kingdom? It is of two kinds. The Kingdom of God is, first of all, on earth. It is the material world of all created things, from the largest to the smallest: the sun, the moon, the stars, the earth, the seas, the land, the trees, the fish, birds, beasts, mankind. God not only brought all these things from nothingness into being, but he continues to govern them. He governs them by means of the laws of nature. If these laws ever stop operating, then the universe will fall to pieces.

The material world is like a huge machine made up of millions of parts, all in their proper place, all moving in order, thus creating the harmony of the universe. If, O man, you admire a machine made by a human being, how much more should you admire the infinitely more complex machine of the universe as created by God? Man's creations are like childrens' toys compared to God's.

And so, man, observing the wonders of the material universe, turns to God and says: "O God, how beautiful is this world you have made! How beautiful the sun, the moon, the stars, the planets, the galaxies; how sweetly smell your multicolored flowers. Blessed be your Kingdom!"

God's Kingdom is also a spiritual kingdom. The spiritual world is the world of angels and archangels, the immaterial beings who live in heaven. These beings obey God, perform His will and sing His eternal glory.

This spiritual kingdom extends into the material. God reigns over His people, who have bodies and so are in the material world, and who have souls and so are in the spiritual world. But which people does He govern? Those who believe in Him, the true God, and do His will, as do the holy angels. God reigns in the hearts of his selected subjects.

We ask: Who is this God? All religions have a God. Our religion, however, differs from all others because we believe in the true God, Whom Christ revealed to the world. The true God is the Triune God, the Father, the Son, and the Holy Spirit; one Divinity in three Persons. Holy Trinity, have mercy on your world and on us sinners.

These three Persons of the Holy Trinity, as the Holy Scriptures teach us, are inseparable. The Father, the Son, and the Holy Spirit are one. And the three Persons work together, according to the Scriptures, for the salvation of man. There is a marvelous harmony in all acts aimed at man's salvation.

The Triune God – Father, Son, and Holy Spirit – illuminates the earth. On earth He shines most brightly in His Church, which Christ, with the Father and the cooperation of the Holy Spirit, came to establish on earth.

Those who believe, experience the grandeur of God's Kingdom, and are grateful to the Triune God. The priest speaks for them: "O Holy Trinity, how beautiful are the wonders Thou hast created." Many, however, have left the Church and have become slaves of satan.

AMEN

In the previous homily, we explained the reading that opens the Divine Liturgy, "Blessed be the Kingdom of the Father, and the Son, and of the Holy Spirit." After the priest has read this aloud, the cantor responds with "Amen." In this homily, we will explain this word, "Amen." Please be attentive, for each word used in the Divine Liturgy has its purpose. Each is like a gold coin, and, as we don't toss gold coins away but rather hold onto them and use them, so must we Christians hold on to this word. Yes, my God, sings the Psalmist David, "in my heart I hid Thy sayings" like a precious treasure (Psalm 118:11).

The word "Amen" is not a Greek one; it is Hebrew. We find it in the Holy Bible, both in the Old and New Testaments, and we hear it in the Divine Liturgy. What does it mean? If the "Amen" begins a sentence, and especially if it is repeated ("Amen, Amen"), this means that what follows is true. Thus, Christ asserts: "Truly, truly I say to you . . ."; "I tell you that my word is true and certain."

When the "Amen" is at the end of a sentence, it may mean the same as it means at the beginning of a sentence, but it may also mean – and this is more common – "so be it," "may that which has been said become real."

In general, this is what "Amen" means. However, when it follows the acclamation: "Blessed be the Kingdom . . .," what does "Amen" mean? Is it affirmative or wishful? Most commentators suggest that "Amen" in this instance is an affirmation. We are of the opinion, however, that it is both an affirmation and a wish. Let us consider this closely.

Let us recall the priest's pronouncement. He begins the Divine Liturgy by proclaiming the existence of the Kingdom of God. To this solemn declaration we add the response of the people, as expressed by the cantor or choir: "Amen," thereby affirming the reality of the Kingdom and its glory. Whoever doubts this is not a Christian. The unbelievers and atheists deny the Kingdom of the Father, the Son, and the Holy Spirit. They believe, as a certain philosopher put it, in another trinity, that of money, flesh, and worldly power.

"But how," ask the unbelievers, "can we believe that three Persons are one?" St. Augustine, one of the famous Fathers of our Church, asked himself the same question. He pondered this great mystery of the Holy Trinity until he felt vertigo. He came out of his room, dazed, and went for a walk along the seashore to clear his head. There he saw a child who had just finished digging a little hole in the sand and was carrying water from the sea in a small pot and pouring it into the hole.

"What are you doing, my child?" asked St. Augustine.

"Do you see all the water in that ocean? I'm going to pour it all into this hole," the child answered.

"But, that's impossible," responded St. Augustine.

"Yet if this is impossible," said the child, "how much more so to do what you are trying to do, to comprehend the mystery of the Holy Trinity."

This was an angel in human form, sent to teach St. Augustine that the mind cannot contain the enormous mystery of the Holy Trinity.

Yes, Lord, I believe. I pay no heed to unbelievers and atheists. I listen to the Holy Gospel. And with the Church, which preserves the true meaning of the Gospel, I believe in and confess the Holy Trinity.

And so, blessed and glorified be the Holy Trinity.

In heaven, dwelling place of angels and archangels, the eternal Holy Trinity is indeed blessed and glorified, for so we are told in the Book of Revelations. But here on earth, is the Holy Trinity blessed and glorified by all the world? Sadly, no. Two-thirds of mankind does not believe in the Gospel. Some continue to worship animal spirits and wild beasts; to reverence the sun, fire, and various natural phenomena; to perform witchcraft and worship satan. Others believe in religions which deny the Holy Trinity.

And even among the one billion people who have been baptized and profess to be Christians, how many truly believe in the Holy Trinity? Among these there are men who not only deny their faith, but blaspheme the Trinity with shameful words. One such man, unfortunately, is our own Nikos Kazantzakis. He wrote many novels and achieved fame in literary circles. Many admire him, and his works have even been presented on Greek television. The "famous" author does not believe in the Holy Trinity, and mocked this great mystery. But you, good Christian, must close your ears to unbelievers. Don't turn on the radio or TV when words of men mocking our Holy Faith are being transmitted. Believe in the Holy Trinity, as taught in the Holy Gospels. When you hear: "Blessed be the Kingdom of the Father . . .," you should be moved to cry out from the bottom of your heart, "Amen!"

Amen. Yes, Lord, I, an unimportant and sinful man, believe in and confess the Holy Trinity, and I sign my name to it. And may I proclaim my belief not only with my mouth but with my heart, that You, the Triune God, are the true God.

Say the Amen for yourself. But say it also for others. Say the Amen as a wish, that those who do not believe in the Holy Trinity may be moved to believe. May no one blaspheme Your holy name. May everyone praise and glorify it. That which we wish will one day come true, as we are told in Revelation. Every nation which worships idols will bow down before the Triune God, and from every heart and mouth will be heard "Amen," as an expression of universal and absolute recognition.

One last word: the "Amen" was not always said only by the cantor or the choir. It used to be said by all the people attending Church. Men, women, and children used to shout with one voice an "Amen" so powerful it seemed like thunder.

O, faith of the first Christians, when will you come again to warm our hearts?

PEACEFUL

"In peace let us pray to the Lord"

After the priest has proclaimed "Blessed be the Kingdom . . ." and the cantor has responded with "Amen," either the priest or the deacon continues: "In peace let us pray to the Lord." Let us examine the implications of this phrase.

Every Orthodox Christian is obligated to go to church every Sunday as well as on major holidays of Christendom, unless sick or otherwise incapable of attending. Church attendance is one of our most sacred duties. But I ask: Is it enough merely to attend church?

In order for church attendance to do good and to bring about its excellent results, it must be done as God wants it done. And what God wants from us when we are at church is evident from Christ's discussion of the matter during His Sermon on the Mount: "So if you are about to offer your gift to God at the altar and there you remember that your brother has something against you, leave your gift in front of the altar and go at once to make peace with your brother; then come back and offer your gift to God" (Matt. 5:23-24). O man, says the Lord, you who come to church to pray and to offer a sacrifice to God – examine yourself. If you know of a man who has a complaint against you, go find him before offering your sacrifice, and, if you have wronged him, ask his forgiveness and be reconciled with him. And thus reconciled and at peace, come back to church and offer your sacrifice. Your gift is unacceptable as long as you have aversion, hatred, and revenge in your heart.

This is the Lord's commandment. The Lord asks all of us to love our fellowmen and be at peace with them. He wants this always, but especially at the hour when the Divine Liturgy is celebrated, the bloodless sacrifice offered. He wants to see us like a family, full of love, gathered around His table.

But perhaps someone will say: "Very well. I know what the Lord says and I want to obey His law. I want to love, and to be at peace with, every man. I am willing to forgive even my greatest enemy, or to ask forgiveness from someone I wronged." Unfortunately, some men are so wicked and malicious that they will not be reconciled with me, even if I am conciliatory and peaceful. These hateful people tell you to your face: "I do not want your love. I do not want forgiveness. I would not forgive you if you prostrated yourself before me a hundred thousand times. I hate you, and will do everything possible to have my revenge. I will persecute you and I will destroy you. I am your enemy and I want you to know it."

There are, sad to say, such hard hearts, which hold on to their hate and long for revenge. In such cases, the Christian who has done his duty is no longer responsible. The man who does not forgive his fellow man is guilty before God. Woe to the hard hearts which are not softened by love.

There is a very moving and instructive example among the martyrs of our Holy Church. Two Christians, Nikephoros and Saprikios, quarreled with each other. It was a time of persecutions. The heathens arrested Saprikios. He confessed Christ and so was to be executed.

Nikephoros learned of it, came to where they held Saprikios, fell at his feet and begged forgiveness. Saprikios, however, despite Nikephoros' prostrations and tears, was unmoved. He would not forgive. And then something terrible happened to him. Saprikios, who had until then confessed Christ, lost his nerve and denied Christ. Divine grace abandoned him, because in his heart he did not love and forgive his brother. When Nikephoros heard Saprikios deny Christ, he himself confessed his faith and suffered martyrdom. God disapproved of the man with the hateful heart and would not accept his sacrifice. And so we learn that God will not accept anything from us so long as we hate in our hearts.

"In peace let us pray to the Lord." Let not our hearts be disturbed during the hour of the Divine Liturgy by feelings of hate and revenge. As much as it is in our power, let us make peace with all people. And even if our enemies hate us, nail us to a cross, spit on us and insult us – even then a true Christian must imitate Christ, pray for his offendors, and ask the heavenly Father: "Forgive them, Father! They do not know what they are doing" (Luke 23:34). We must have peace in our hearts even when we are wounded by all the injustices of the world. Peace with all men. The peace of Christ.

"In peace let us pray to the Lord." We must pray peacefully in God's House. Do all? Unfortunately, no. Hate fills the hearts of many. And still these men who hate each other come to church as if nothing important is happening. They say that they attend church, but can this really be attending church? In the same church are people who do not speak to each other outside of the church. Often these people are relatives and friends. They enter the church full of hate and leave it full of hate. Christ's peace has left their hearts and the devil's hate reigns there instead. Let them know that they gain nothing, regardless of how much they offer or how many candles they light. For they lack the most important thing: peace and love. Let us attend to the priest when he says: "In peace let us pray to the Lord."

THE LAST SUPPER

SHORT PRAYER

"Lord, have mercy"

We are explaining the great supplication, which is, as we have said, a series of prayers directed by the priest to the Triune God. Each of the prayers begins with the word "For" and ends with "let us pray to the Lord." After each petition, the cantor adds: "Lord have mercy."

"Lord, have mercy" is the shortest prayer of our Church, a petition of three words. This prayer, however, performs miracles. And it is this prayer which is the subject of this homily.

Let us consider two examples, one from the Old Testament and the other from the New. The Old Testament example is from the First Book of Kings. This book tells of a pious woman named Anna who lived about 1100 B.C. She was married to a man who loved her very much. But Anna's heart was full of sorrow. She had no children. She prayed to God to give her a child. One day she went to church and stayed there all day, praying: "My God and my Lord, have mercy on me. Do not forsake me. Give me a child, and I will dedicate this child to thy service." She did not say this prayer aloud, but in her heart, which was inflamed by faith in God. Anyone who saw her, kneeling, tears in her eyes, her lips moving but making no sound, would have thought her delirious.

A priest, named Eli, saw Anna and thought she was drunk. Yes, she was drunk, but not from wine of the vine, but from the wine of contrition. Holy contrition is the experience of grief that comes from feeling oneself unworthy before God, and this holy woman experienced this grief in her prayers.

The priest thought that Anna was drunk. But her short prayer, the equivalent of our "Lord, have mercy," performed its miracle. She, the barren woman, gave birth to a child, a brilliant child, who was to become a great prophet of Israel. There was a time, long ago, when children were conceived through the ardent prayers of their parents, while today the seeds are sown in drunkenness and debauchery. Children born from such unholy unions, more often than not, grow to have terrible vices and defects, magnifying the wretched and criminal lives of their parents. But let us return to Anna. In response to her short prayer, a miracle took place. She became the mother of Samuel (I King 1:1-12).

Let us turn now to the New Testament. Open to the Gospel according to St. Matthew, and read about another woman, the Canaanite. She came from a country whose inhabitants did not believe in the true God, but practiced sorcery and worshipped idols. When this woman learned, however, that Christ had crossed the borders into her country, she believed in Him, and believed more profoundly than did the Hebrews. She came to Christ, begging Him to cure her daughter, who was possessed by a demon and had been pronounced incurable by Canaanite doctors and magicians. This woman came to Christ and cried out: "O Lord, son of David, have mercy on me; my daughter is severely possessed by a demon." She cried once, twice, many times, "Lord, have mercy," but Christ did not answer her request. And when Christ, to test her faith, said that the father does not give the bread that is intended for the children to the dogs, this courageous woman humbly answered: "O Lord, I do not ask for the bread meant for the children, but, like a dog, I beg for one crumb of your infinite mercy, which you distribute to the world. One crumb is enough for me. O Lord, have mercy." And the Lord performed His miracle. He fulfilled the woman's request by healing her daughter (Matt. 15:22-28).

"Lord, have mercy," said Anna, and she gave birth to a child. "Lord, have mercy," cried the Canaanite woman, and her daughter was cured. "Lord, have mercy," begged the ten lepers, and they were cleansed of their awful illness. "Lord, have mercy," the Christians of the ancient Church used to say all together, and their short prayer worked wonders.

Today, instead of everyone responding to the priest's petitions, only the cantor says "Lord, have mercy." It should once again be said by all who attend the services. One "Lord, have mercy," offered from the bottom of the heart of the faithful, is worth more than many long prayers said without faith and with an unclean heart.

Before closing, let me pass on to you this anecdote on the power of: "Lord, have mercy." Once upon a time there lived on the mountainside a shepherd and his son. When the son had grown to be a man, he told his father, "I'm sick and tired of raising sheep. I want to be a king." He left his father and the flock and headed for the big city in hopes of becoming king. On his way to the city he met a magician, and he told him of his longing. The magician said: "I'll give you a piece of paper. Take it to the cemetery at midnight, throw it on the graves, and wait. Somebody will come. Don't be afraid. He is the governor of the world. He will make you king." The young shepherd took the magic paper, went to the cemetery at night, and waited. Midnight came. He threw the paper. Just then he heard sounds, like howling of wolves and jackals. And he saw, coming towards him, the devil! The poor shepherd shook with fear. In this moment of panic, he remembered his mother, who told him that if he was ever in danger, he should cry aloud: "Lord, have mercy." And he did just that. He fell to his knees and cried: "Lord, have mercy." The howling stopped. The devil disappeared.

Next day, he sought out the magician, who gave him more advice. "You must go again," he told the boy, "to the cemetery, and you must throw this paper on the graves. But first you must kill an innocent child which you will find on the road, cut out its heart, and bring it to me. Will you do this?" The shepherd hesitated for a while, and then gave in. He carried out his orders. He killed a child, brought the heart to the magician, took the paper from him, and by midnight was once again in the cemetery. Again he threw the paper, and again the demon appeared, and again the shepherd lost courage. He dropped to his knees and began praying: "Lord, have mercy," once, twice, hundreds, and thousands of times. This time the demon did not disappear.

The first time, one "Lord, have mercy" made the demon vanish. The second time, a thousand had no effect. I shall not explain. You understand. You know when God hears "Lord, have mercy" and when He does not.

WHERE IS PEACE?

"For the peace from above . . . let us pray to the Lord."

Once the congregation has been urgently asked to pray in peace, the priest begins a series of petitions to God. These petitions are joined together to form a golden chain which unites us with heaven. All together these petitions are called the great supplication.

The first prayer, "For the peace from above"; the second, "For the salvation of our souls". In this homily we will once again discuss peace, and particularly its source.

"Peace" is one of the most loved words in any language. There is no man, no matter where he may live or what language he may speak, who does not want peace. Individuals want peace. Families want peace. Cities and nations want peace. Mankind wants peace.

"Peace" is a sweet word, a sweeter reality. If anyone were to sit in on a session of the United Nations, he would hear orators of all nations speaking on a range of subjects, and he would note that the most often repeated word is peace. This word has been recorded countless times in the minutes of these sessions. No nation seems to want war. Each, from the least significant to the super powers, with their stockpiles of nuclear weapons, claims it wants peace. But what is this peace that great and small alike seek?

The wild beasts of the African jungle, when hungry, leave their lairs to hunt, catch, kill, and eat smaller animals. After they have eaten the flesh they have torn apart with their terrible claws and teeth, they retreat to their lairs, their mouths bathed in blood, pacified, to rest. These do not bother anyone when they are satiated. But when they feel again the pangs of hunger, once more they charge out of their lairs, bellowing and ready to war against smaller, weaker animals. The mighty and powerful states of this world act in the same way. They are like the wild beasts in the Revelation of St. John that come from the center of the abyss of evil. These mighty nations, these wild beasts, wage war against smaller nations. They defeat them, tear them to pieces, steal from them, exploit them, and they call this period of cheating and exploitation "peace." When they get hungry for more, they will again war against new victims, for new spoils.

This "peace," based on violence, crimes, and injustice, is not the peace of God. It is the peace of this world. In ancient times, the Roman Empire fought and conquered all nations and imposed on them its authority. And this compulsory subjugation of all peoples to Rome's sceptre was called "peace." *Pax Romana!* None of the conquered, the enslaved, dared to claim their rights. The Roman banner waved proudly everywhere.

Something like this is going to happen in our own time. The three or four superpowers are like the wild beasts of Revelation. They continuously speak of peace, but continuously prepare for war. Their war will be the worst war of all time. They do not care how much blood will be shed, how much of the world they will destroy. One thing alone interests them, and they will fight for it fiercely, savagely, like the lion and the tiger in the jungle. They will not fight for liberty and justice, as their diplomats claim. They will fight for oil. They will fight for raw materials. And whichever beast wins this war will declare supremacy over all others and so announce the universal peace. But this peace, stained with the world's blood, will be as far removed from true peace, as a counterfeit coin is from gold. For the true peace is not of this world, but of heaven.

Is there, indeed, a peace from above? Truly, there is. The angels sang of this peace on the unforgetable night of our Savior's birth, singing: "Glory to God in the highest, and on earth peace, good will toward men" (Luke 2:14). Christ gave His disciples this peace, saying: "Peace I leave with you, my peace I give unto you. Not as the world giveth, give I unto you. Let not your heart be troubled, neither let it be afraid" (John 14:27).

I give you, says Christ, my peace. My peace differs from the peace of the world. It is an internal peace. It is a peace which reaches the depths of the human heart and cleanses it from evil and passions, making man truly free and happy.

O peace of Christ! This peace was sealed with the blood of the God-Man on Golgotha. On that hill, heaven and earth were reconciled. There man and God met in the infinite mystery of Christ's sacrifice. Through His cross, we are delivered. Through His cross is true victory and peace.

Peace, then, is from above, from heaven. And it is for this peace, whose source is Christ, that our Church prays: "For the peace from above . . . let us pray to the Lord."

But who is there today who believes in this peace of Christ? Whatever our Church preaches concerning this peace seems incomprehensible to this corrupt and unfaithful world. The people of our time live only for the peace of the world. That is, they want to live without fear, without hunger and misery, without worries, wars, and revolutions. They want a peace that will let them enjoy their material goods; that will let them eat, drink, and amuse themselves with animal pleasures; that will let them live without any thought about God. But this is not the peace which the man who is conscious of his divine destiny seeks. Such a man, who is not completely corrupted by sin, feels within himself an evil which neither he himself, nor any other man, can cure. He knows that only by Divine grace can this evil be crushed and defeated and his wounds healed. Such a man knows that only then will he be truly free, redeemed, at peace.

This evil is sin which never stops torturing man. The forgiveness of sins, deliverance from their tyranny, is brought on by the inner peace, the peace of Christ. His peace is not a dream, but a reality, which is enjoyed by those who earnestly believe and repent.

THE SALVATION OF OUR SOULS

"For the salvation of our souls, let us pray to the Lord"

We continue, beloved in Christ, with our explanation of the great supplication. In the previous homily we considered the first petition: "For the peace from above." Today, we are concerned with the second petition: "For the salvation of our souls."

Man is constituted of body and soul. No one disputes the fact that he has a body. It can be seen, handled, and analyzed in scientific laboratories. The body is of great value. It is a wondrous organism, which can operate for up to 100 or more years. The bodily organism is made up of many parts, each indispensable for the body's normal functioning. Each part, among which are the eyes, ears, lungs, kidneys, liver, spleen, and heart, as well as many others, has its own specific function. Some of these parts are irreplaceable. Science, it is true, has succeeded in artificially reproducing certain organs, but these replacements can not compare in perfection with our natural organs.

The body, as we are taught in the New Testament, is a temple of God. A temple made of stone is not valuable in and of itself, because of its materials and its artistic design, but because it is where man worships God. So with the human body. The body is valuable because it is the dwelling-place of the soul.

"Is there a soul?" men ask. "We see the body. We do not see the soul. Where is this soul?" The soul, we answer, is immaterial, and as such is invisible. Yet, even though it is invisible, no reasonable man can deny its existence. The proof is in its many manifestations, which can only be explained as the actions of the soul within the body. It is not the body but the soul which thinks, judges, perceives, feels, is conscious, exercises free choice, all of which makes man like a small God on earth. These qualities of the soul – intellect, free will, conscience – distinguish man from all other animals. The man who properly uses these divine gifts can attain heights of virtue, and become like an angel, differing only in that he will still have a body. He will be an angel in the flesh. But the man who misuses these gifts will fall into sin, become corrupt, bestial, demonic, an incarnate devil.

Man has a soul. And because this soul is so precious, man should be infinitely more concerned for its well-being than for the well-being of his body. Sadly, however, man today has turned all his attention to his body, to the corporeal and material needs. He concerns himself with the body – how to make it work better, how to make it live longer, how to make it enjoy every earthly pleasure. He talks of everything except the soul. It is as if the soul does not exist.

Consider these two examples. A man takes ill. He is told that he can only be healed abroad, in England or America. Regardless of how poor he may be, this man will do whatever he can to get there. We do not accuse the man of being concerned for his body's health. But we ask: Is it only the body that gets sick? Is the soul never ill? Are not the evils that live and breed in the innermost depths of man, such as greed, lust, envy, hatred, and wrath, horrible diseases, more dreadful than any that inflict the flesh? Should not the man seek out a doctor that can cure him?

There is - glory to God - such a doctor! The only supreme, almighty doctor of souls and bodies is our Lord Jesus Christ. You can meet this doctor in His clinic. His private sanitarium is His holy Church. And yet the man who sacrifices everything to travel abroad for medical attention does not take a single step towards the healing of his soul. Just think of how many are living without confession! Every effort is made to heal the body, yet nothing is done for the soul.

But this body which we handle with such care will one day fade away and die. And, like the body, all material things which the world admires are doomed to destruction. What will remain? A single powerful earth-quake lasting only a few seconds can level entire cities. What will survive world-wide destruction? What will remain? The soul will remain. As will Christ — He who created it, He who will judge it.

Imagine an enormous set of scales, suspended from the stars and visible all over the world. Imagine that on one side of the scale the material wealth of the world is piled high, and that on the other side there is only a single soul, not of a great and famous man, but of the poorest and most unfortunate man of the earth. Imagine this soul is like a winged angel, flying towards the scale. If only the tip of its wings brushed the scale, it would tip in the soul's favor, even though all the riches of the world were amassed on the other side. Does a man gain anything if he wins the whole world but loses his soul?

Of course not! There is nothing a man can give to win back his soul (Mark 8:36-37).

The most important of all subjects, then, is the salvation of our souls. Our souls must be saved. Woe to the soul that is not saved. Eternal damnation awaits it. And so the priest, immediately after the beginning of the Divine Liturgy, and before any other petition, admonishes us to ask for peace and for the salvation of our souls: "For the peace from above and the salvation of our souls, let us pray to the Lord."

UNIVERSAL PEACE

"For the peace of the whole world . . . let us pray to the Lord."

Man, my dear ones, is not self-sufficient. Regardless of how powerful he may be, he alone cannot satisfy his needs, material or spiritual. He needs and seeks help from others. He petitions authorities at various levels of government for the satisfaction of his requests. If his requests are ignored at one level, he bows before the most influential people in hopes that they will hear his pleas and grant him satisfaction.

Yet, as we have emphasized in previous homilies, there exists beyond all earthly authorities and governments an ultimate authority, a supreme governor. This is the Holy Trinity: Father, Son, and Holy Spirit. The Holy Trinity governs the entire universe and is infinitely powerful. The Holy Trinity is the true God, Whom we venerate and worship. The Divine Liturgy begins with an invocation of the Holy Trinity. If worldly authorities, often cruel and inhuman, can be moved by frequent and fervent requests to satisfy the petitioner, we can be certain that our Triune God, who is all love, will deign to answer our prayers as long as what we ask for is in our eternal interest.

God is our Father. What father, asks Christ, would answer his child's request for bread with a stone, or for fish with a serpent? (Matt. 7:9-10). If a father in the flesh is compassionate and loves his child, imagine how much more God loves us. He is our good father. Let us pray to Him and direct to Him our requests. One of the links, the third link, of the chain of petitions which man in his weakness offers to his all-powerful God during the Divine Liturgy and after the invocation of the Holy Trinity, is this: *"For the peace of the whole world, the stability of the Holy Churches of God, and for the unity of all mankind, let us pray to the Lord."* With this petition, we ask three things of God: universal peace, stability of the Churches, and union of all men. This homily is about the first of these requests.

Peace! We petition the Lord for universal peace. God's peace, the peace that reigns in His heavenly realm of angels and saints, is a profound and lasting peace, undisturbed by discord. Countless angels obey the Triune God, praising Him with song and glorifying Him unceasingly. Only once, according to Scripture, did there occur a great disturbance in this heavenly kingdom. On that occasion, one of the archangels, who shone with the brilliance of the morning star, Lucifer, took pride in himself, and imagining that he could transcend God Himself, declared rebellion against Him and convinced a number of his fellow angels to join in the rebellion. This resulted in Lucifer and his armies being thrown from heaven like a lightning bolt. They remain today the demons, the enemies of God's will. The bulk of angels, however, remained faithful and obedient to God. They continue to enjoy His full and infinite peace.

On our earth, however, on this small planet of this immense universe, is there peace? In spite of all, there is indeed peace on earth. It is the peace within, which only a few enjoy. They are the people who believe in

Christ. You, too, my dear fellow Christian, can share in this rare and priceless blessing, this peace. To do so, you must first call to mind your sins, sincerely repent, have faith that Jesus Christ forgives all the sins of men, confess and ask for forgiveness of your spiritual father, who represents Christ, and then, in the depths of your heart, you will hear a secret voice saying: "Your sins have been forgiven. You are the beloved child of God." It will be the voice of Christ, addressed to every repentant sinner: "Take heart, my son, your sins are forgiven" (Matt. 9:2).

From the moment the sinner is assured that his sins are forgiven, his troubled concience is pacified. Peace reigns in his heart – an inexpressible, indescribable peace, which can be enjoyed by whoever repents and believes in Christ. This is the peace within.

Whoever, therefore, sincerely repents and believes in Christ can enjoy this priceless gift of peace. And yet, he does not rest quietly from then on. A holy uneasiness takes hold of him. A holy longing invades his inner self. He wants the holy blessing, which he himself enjoys, to be enjoyed by all men. As a man who has discovered an oasis in the middle of the desert first quenches his own thirst and then runs to tell others of his find and to lead them to refreshment, so the Christian who drinks from the source of peace, which is Christ, calls out to all those spiritually thirsty to drink from this spring and be at peace.

The Christian is the bearer of the Good News, of peace to the world. There is no doubt that if all who call themselves Christians become true Christians, preaching Christ's gospel of peace to all the world by word and by deed, all people, regardless of race and language, would believe in Christ. Then peace would embrace the world, and all would be one. Only by preaching and living the message of the Gospel will the world come to know universal peace.

O how very, very distant does this day of universal peace seem! Yet, let not the faithful stop praying and working for this peace to come to all.

THE TEMPEST-TOSSED CHURCH

"For the stability of the Holy Churches of God, let us pray to the Lord."

The history of the Church of Christ, how it was established and how it spread throughout the world, is a miracle of the greatest magnitude. Church history bears witness that the Church is a heavenly tree, planted by the Holy Trinity, a tree which no satanic force will ever be able to uproot. Let us consider one of the countless inspiring episodes of the Church's expansion.

On a tiny island, far off the Pacific Ocean, there lived savages who had never heard about Christ. These pagans offered human sacrifices to their gods. One day, there came to this island a missionary, whose desire was to preach the Gospel in lands where Christ's message had not yet been heard. He had been miraculously washed ashore onto the island after his ship had sunk in a storm at sea. The missionary finally succeeded, after much effort, in converting a single native, who professed belief in Christ and was baptized. The missionary thanked and glorified God, for he was no longer the sole believer on the island. Before long, the native had convinced a friend of the truth of the Gospel, and soon there were three Christians, who together founded the island's first Church of Christ. Soon the entire island, all its men, women, and children, saw the light and were baptized into the Church.

In like fashion, the faith spread throughout the world. To idolatrous, corrupt, and sinful peoples, zealous preachers brought the Good News, and amongst them established the first Churches. The first preachers of the Gospel, the Apostles, were unrivalled in their persuasive power and authority. The Apostle Paul was particularly active throughout the Mediterranean world, establishing Churches in many major cities. In Greece, Churches were founded in Philippi, Thessaloniki, Verroia, Athens, Corinth and Crete. In Asia Minor, many Churches, including the seven mentioned in the Book of Revelation, were established. These particular Churches, which shone like heavenly stars on earth, no longer exist. They were all destroyed. But those Christians who survived the Turkish persecutions escaped to Greece, where they were admitted into the Churches of Greece. And those Orthodox Christians who were forced abroad, for whatever reasons, wherever they went, established Orthodox Churches. And so today there are Churches in America, Germany, France, Asia, Australia, and Africa.

It seems as if there are many churches throughout the cities and countries. No matter how many individual church buildings and communities there may be, in reality each member of each church has been baptized according to the doctrines of the Orthodox faith, and so all stand steadfast in the one true faith. All these churches, wherever they may be, and in whichever language they may celebrate the Divine Liturgy and administer the sacraments, constitute one Church. It is the one, holy, catholic and apostolic Church. As the body is one, governed by the head, so the Church of Christ is one body, with Jesus Christ as our head and the Orthodox faithful as the body's members. That is, all members of the Church share a common doctrine and moral teaching, and are governed by the clergy, bishops, and archbishops. The Orthodox Church is spread throughout most of the world. Its spiritual centers are the four ancient Patriarchates of Constantinople, Alexandria, Jerusalem, and Antioch, as well as the autonomous Churches of Russia, Greece, Bulgaria, etc. All together, these Patriarchates and autonomous Churches constitute the one, holy, catholic and apostolic Church.

The Orthodox Church is like a ship which has been at sea now for centuries. Huge waves strike the ship's sides and threaten to sink it. These are the waves of error and heresy which have often attacked the true faith. These are also the waves of savage persecution by which corrupt and faithless powers have tried to violently suppress and in fact exterminate Orthodoxy. And those who experience these horrid persecutions fear that the time of the Church's destruction has come.

And yet, in spite of all, the Orthodox Church remains afloat. It may be tossed by the sea, as a great Church Father has observed, but it cannot sink. Look at the Church in Russia. There, an atheist regime, which publicly proclaims atheism, has tried for years to destroy the Church. It has persecuted priests, shut down churches and monasteries, and has mercilessly tortured Christians. And yet, the Church survives. It lives on in the hearts of countless Russians, who believe in God and in Orthodoxy, and who congregate wherever they can to worship their God with fervor. They worship as did the Christians of the catacombs.

It is our duty as Christians to keep in mind those Orthodox Churches throughout the world that are threatened by deadly enemies, that are plagued with difficulties. For these Churches, the Divine Liturgy calls us to pray. Let us ask Christ to grant strength to those Churches, so that, firm in the Orthodox faith, they may overcome their trials and emerge victorious.

Brothers and sisters in Christ, for the stability of the holy Churches of God, let us pray to the Lord.

CHRISTIANS, UNITE!

"For the union of all, let us pray to the Lord."

We ask the Triune God, in the last part of the second petition of the great supplication, for the union of all. Of this union, we will here speak.

That we may see how great a blessing is Christian unity, let us consider an example. Somewhere there is a village of no more than one hundred families. All the villagers - men, women, and children - have been baptized in the name of the Holy Trinity. All are Orthodox Christians. They are blessed with an excellent priest, who has lived with them for years, and who, like a good shepherd, never tires of attending to the needs of his flock. And so, Christianity thrives in every household. Parents love their children, and children respect their parents. If ever a misunderstanding flares up between families, the peace of God returns to their homes. All are united. There isn't a heretic, nor an unbeliever, among them.

In this village, all are as one. They rejoice with the happy and weep with the sad. They are one hundred different families, and yet they are one big family. Christ is the head of this family. The inhabitants of the village are all Christ's chosen children. And the priest acts as Christ in caring for his people's material and spiritual needs.

Darkness fell over the land. The satan of separateness, the demon of divisions succeeded in splitting many neighboring villages apart; but nothing happened to this village. All remained united. The village stood, an uncaptured citadel.

What a blessing it is to be a united village! Do not suppose that this example is mere fiction. There are today, in our own country - glory to God! - many such villages which have preserved their Christian faith and unity. There are, within the boundaries of our own metropolis, which by God's mercy I serve as bishop, certain small villages wherein I experience inexpressible joy whenever I celebrate the Divine Liturgy. The people of these villages come to church like members of the same beloved family, and they attend with great attention and reverence. They do not hate one another. They never take anyone to court. They do not steal from each other. Of course I do not mean to say that they are perfect Christians, for perfection is a rare attainment found only in saints. But, with respect to our theme of unity, these villages are indeed one in faith, united.

How many such villages are there? Of our country's 10,000 villages and towns, how many can claim this remarkable unity? Alas, only a very few. And with the passing years, yielding to satan's influence, evil spreads like a plague, turning neighbor against neighbor. The faithful villages are getting fewer and fewer. Satan has the upper hand these days. He stands holding a sledgehammer, ready to smash to bits the beautiful mirror of unity.

We have discussed life in a united village. Let us now turn our attention to a village divided against itself. Its inhabitants disagree in matters of faith and morals. Satan's agents are everywhere. One poses as a materialist and atheist, arguing that there is no God, that heaven and hell are fantasies. Another pretends to believe in Christ but claims that the Church's teachings are not applicable to today's problems, that change is necessary. A third, masquerading as a doctor of science, tells the villagers that they must practice birth control, that virginity is old-fashioned and out-moded, that a new age is dawning without religious restrictions and superstitions. A fourth, an immigrant from America infected with the disease of the Jehovah Witnesses, distributes pamphlets and money, making himself to be an angel of the Lord in the eyes of some villagers and convincing them to join him in his satanic heresy.

The villagers were not attentive to the dangers inherent in listening to such anti-Christian heresies. They did not have a compassionate priest to protect them from the wolves. These poor people, without the guidance of a good and strong leader, fell one after another into the traps set for them by satan's agents. One became an atheist, another a Protestant, another a blasphemer, and so on. And so the village, which had been united in faith before the coming of satan's agents, fell to pieces, with no two men sharing the same faith. There were as many different beliefs as there were people.

And the same goes on in the big cities. City residents are no more united than villagers, and in fact are divided into even more factions. These factions hate each other and try to dominate by means of violence and deceit. The world is deeply divided, as never before.

This division has even penetrated the Church! The unity for which Christ prayed on Great Thursday evening, the unity of the first Christians which elicited such admiration from pagans and non-believers, the unity

with which Christians of the past confronted every dif-
ficulty - this unity is no more! Our hierarchy is divided,
our clergy is divided, our laity is divided. Wolves have
entered the fold and have scattered the flock. The
shepherds must now labor to track down the dispersed
sheep, carrying each on their shoulders back to Christ's
fold.

We must all join the priest in asking God for this
union: "For the union of all, let us pray to the Lord."

THE HOUSE OF GOD

"For this holy house . . ., let us pray to the Lord."

The third petition of the great supplication, addressed by the priest to God at the beginning of the Divine Liturgy, asks two things of God: first, that He bless His holy house, and second, that He bless those who attend services in it. Let us concentrate for now on the first of the two requests.

"For this holy house." We have mentioned in the past that God as Spirit is everywhere. Whether man climbs the highest mountains or descends into the deepest seas, or even if he flies to the moon and, beyond that, to the stars, God is there, seeing and hearing everything. For this reason the Psalmist says: "In every place of His dominion, bless the Lord, O my soul" (102:21). Even in prison, a man can communicate with God through the secret transmitter called "prayer." Anyone who has read the lives of the martyrs knows that those Christians who were arrested for their beliefs and sentenced to death by idolators, while in prison, awaiting their execution, prayed more fervently, more sincerely, more beautifully than ever before in their lives.

Man's body, as well as the entire universe, is, we are taught by Apostle Paul, the temple of God (I Cor. 3:16). The soul which abides in this temple, which believes in and reveres God, can pray at every moment.

It can pray silently, without being heard by anyone. Its prayer ascends into heaven as if it had angelic wings.

Perhaps someone listening will say to himself: "If I can pray to God anywhere and everywhere, then why do I have to go to church?" It's sad that so many people have been so strongly influenced by groups like Jehovah's Witnesses. These people never go to church, and don't even cross themselves when passing by a church or chapel.

Our response to them is: Christ, during His ministry on earth, did not preach the abolishment of houses of prayer. Indeed, He did teach us to pray at all times and all places, but He also taught, besides private prayer, the public prayer of many people congregated in one place. He Himself, when He was twelve years old, went to the temple in Jerusalem; He so loved that temple that He stayed there for three days, praying and discussing Mosaic Law with priests and rabbis, eliciting awe and admiration from all who heard Him speak. When His holy Mother, who had lost Him and sought Him for three days, finally discovered Him in the temple, He told her: "Didn't you know that I had to be in my Father's house?" (Luke 2:49).

In another instance, when He was forced to drive the moneylenders from the temple which they had turned into a marketplace, Christ called the temple "a house of prayer," and not "a den of thieves" (Matt. 21:13). It is clear, therefore, that Christ did not abolish the temple as a place of public worship. My fellow Christians, you must pray to God wherever you may be, at home or at work, but you must not think this excuses you from attending church every Sunday and holiday, along with all of God's people.

The church is a place distinguished from all other places, because it is dedicated solely to prayer. Everything about the church, from the art and architecture of the building itself to the words said and the actions performed within the building, contributes to an environment of holy contrition, wherein those who attend church services can be mystically elevated to the throne of God. The church houses the sacred vessels, the baptismal font, the censer, the icons, and most importantly the holy altar. On the altar rest the greatest treasures: the Holy Gospels and the holy Chalice. And every time the priest officiates and the mystery of the Divine Eucharist is celebrated, the faithful are invited to receive Holy Communion.

When the priest of the Most High officiates, the church becomes heaven, and though the people present have their feet on the ground, their souls are in heavenly worlds, worshipping in spirit and in truth the Triune God (John 4:23). As we chant the Church's beautiful hymns, "although we are in the temple of His glory, we think that we stand in heaven."

And so the sacred churches have been and continue to be the most beloved of places for those souls in love with God. Together with the Psalmist, they say: "How beloved are Thy dwellings, O Lord of Hosts; my soul longeth and fainteth for the courts of the Lord" (Psalm 8:2-3).

But even though these sacred churches are loved by pious people, who express their love with offerings, these same churches are hated by unbelievers and atheists, who are so evil that the mere sound of church bells infuriates them.

History testifies that whenever idolators and atheists are in power, they destroy churches, desecrate baptismal fonts and holy vessels and kill priests and faithful lay people. This is true not only of the past but of our time as well. Even today there are atheistic states which persecute the Christian faith and by various satanic means try to close the churches and wipe out the Christian population. Just look to our neighbor, Albania, where horrible persecutions have been enacted against Christians. Services are no longer held in the beautiful churches of Korytsa, Argyrokastron, and other cities of Northern Epiros. They have been shut down, and many have been turned into museums, theaters, and storehouses! Their horrible hatred of God makes these men hate everything that reminds them of God, especially the churches.

"For this holy house . . ." All Christians must join in asking God to protect His churches from destruction. And certainly God will hear our prayers and save our churches, if everyone goes to church and attends with the reverence God demands. We will speak of these people in our next homily.

THE CONGREGATION

"For those who enter it with faith, reverence, and the fear of God, let us pray to the Lord."

In our last homily, we discussed the first part of the petition, "For this holy House . . ." We mentioned that there are many unbelievers who want to destroy all our churches. But the faithful Christians, who love the church, pray to God to protect it from every desecration. And God will protect the churches as long as Christians attend services as God wants them attended.

Unfortunately, it is not only the admitted unbelievers who work to destroy the Church. There are many who profess belief in God but who do not live according to this belief. They desecrate the sanctity of the church by their presence. The Jews, for instance, claimed they believed in the true God, and for His worship built the most splendid temple of the world, the temple of Jerusalem. They did not, however, revere this temple. They were disrespectful within its walls as well as without. They used to exchange monies and sell animals for sacrifice within the temple's courts.

These activities angered Christ, and He chased the businessmen out, saying that God's house is a place of prayer and not a market place, "a den of thieves" (John 2:16, Matt. 21:13). Did the Jews understand Christ's criticism? Sadly, no. They continued in their unholy activities and ultimately committed the gravest of crimes, executing the One who had so sternly rebuked them. Even after Christ's crucifixion, the God-Man's murderers continued to go to the temple, their hands dripping with His blood, to offer their sacrifices! But God did not long delay His wrath. Forty years after Christ's crucifixion, the Roman armies came, saw, and conquered Jerusalem, massacred the Jews, and burned the temple to the ground. And so Christ's prophecy, that there would remain of the temple not so much as one stone on top of the other (Matt. 24:2), was fulfilled. As of today, the Jews have not succeeded in rebuilding this temple.

The destruction of the temple of Jerusalem, which was a result of the sins of the Jews, is a warning to us Christians, that in order to enjoy our mighty God's protection, we must treat our churches as places of worship and respect them.

We ask: Do we, the contemporary Christians, clergy and laity, respect the sacred temple? The answer is a disturbing one. Take a look and see what goes on every Sunday and holiday, when the church bell calls the faithful together to worship. As soon as the bell is rung, everyone, with the exception of the very old and sick, should hasten to church. And yet, how very few actually do! The priest begins, the hexapsalmos ("the six psalms") is read, the orthros continues to its end, the doxology is sung, the Divine Liturgy begins, the Gospel is read, the great entrance takes place, and at last people begin wandering into church.

And how do they come? Men smoke their cigarettes until they reach the doors of the church, and then wait to finish their smoke before coming in. They make a hasty and improper sign of the cross. They talk amongst themselves, criticizing the priest and cantor. And they leave before the service is over, lacking even the patience to wait in line for antidoron. Yet how can they accept antidoron when they did not fast and when their mouths are still full of cigarette smoke? During the summer, some men come improperly dressed, in short-sleeve shirts, looking as if they are attending some worldly entertainment and not church.

And women? They, too, dress improperly, immodestly. When they are chastised, they not only fail to recognize their impieties, but they are impertinent and abusive to the priests and bishops who would restrict them. They want to be absolutely free, as they are when they go to parties or to the beach. Especially on islands and in coastal cities frequented by tourists, the impudence of these women has become so great that they dare to enter Church in their short pants! There is no longer any difference, it would seem, between the holy church and a common tavern.

Even those who serve the church, the priest, the chanters, church board members, and custodians, with few exceptions, do not behave as they should. Their actions are improper. The candle stands are busy even at the most sacred moments of the Divine Liturgy. The trustees pass the trays whenever they want. The chanters do not chant with modesty and precision. The priests do not attend their duties with the required reverence. Even the children misbehave, allowed by their parents to run and play in the aisles. Indeed, it is a painful situation.

It would be an overstatement to suggest that this goes on in every church. Happily, that's not the case. In our own diocese, severe measures have been taken and the abuses are now strictly limited. Men in short-sleeved shirts and indecently dressed women are not allowed to enter our churches. And yet, though we have successfully checked certain improprieties, we cannot claim to have achieved the heights demanded of true Orthodox worship. Each priest must work to insure that order, decency, reverence and contrition prevail in our churches.

We twentieth-century Christians can not even imagine how seriously the Christians of the first centuries celebrated the Divine Liturgy. History records many moving examples of their piety, such as the following. St. Basil the Great was celebrating the Divine Liturgy in Caesarea, Asia Minor, for a congregation of devout, contrite, and attentive Christians, when a state official, an unbeliever with bad intentions, entered the church. This official was so impressed by the reverence of everyone present, the laity as well as the clergy, that he had a change of heart, and acknowledged within this church that the true God was indeed worshipped.

My dear brothers in Christ! It is not enough to go to church. We must attend with faith, reverence, and fear of God. With faith that the church is "the house of God." With reverence, with tears of gratitude that God allows us to approach Him in the church. With fear, because we are sinners, deserving punishment. God hates sin, hypocrisy, lies, and the celebrations of those who worship Him with their lips only. With their hearts- alas! - they worship the devil.

Let us be careful! The Church, as the petition reveals, prays only for those who attend church services with faith, reverence, and fear of God.

THE PIOUS AND ORTHODOX CHRISTIANS

"For the pious and Orthodox Christians let us pray to the Lord."

The previous petition was for those Christians who attend their parish church with faith, reverence, and fear of God. Such Christians are few, although there are many who call themselves Orthodox Christians. There are about 200 million Orthodox Christians all over the world. The Church extends its love to all these Christians, and through the priest invites them all to come together to pray for each other.

"For the pious and Orthodox Christians . . .." This petition does not include all Christians without exception, but only the pious ones. Why is there such a restriction? In the first centuries of Christianity, when Christians actually practiced what they preached, the name "Christian" designated all that was good in man. The Christians were, in those years, the light of the world. We read in the lives of the martyrs that when heathens arrested a Christian and asked him his name, his country, and his profession, the arrested man answered simply: "I am a Christian." The word "Christian" was not at that time an empty word. To be a Christian meant, and still means, that a man believes that Christ is the true God, the saviour and redeemer of the whole world. There were only a few Christians in those early years, but they were true to their luminous word, and by their holy example they overcame all obstacles, defeating pagan philosophers and orators, converting kings and emperors, conquering the whole pagan world, raising Christ's flag in every major city of the Roman Empire.

To simply be called a Christian in those days meant that a man was truly a follower of Christ.

However, with the passing of time, after Christianity became the dominant religion throughout the Mediterranean world, men who had no clear idea about what it meant to have faith in Christ and lead a Christian life entered the Church. For reasons of self-interest, they claimed to believe, were baptized, assumed Christian names, and presented themselves as Christians.

But what kind of Christians were they? As a counterfeit coin shines like gold outside, but inside is only cheap metal, so these Christians wore the brightness of the Christian name and reputation, but did not live the reality. Hypocrisy and deceit tarnished the reputation of Christianity.

So today we distinguish between those who call themselves "Christians", and the true Christians, by the word "pious." By "pious Christian," we mean one who is indeed virtuous, full of faith, hope, and love. For these honest and constant Christians, and not for Christians in name only, the Church prays.

It is true that throughout history there have been men called Christians who were not bound in essence to Christ. They were hypocrites and traitors. This is especially true today, and the Christian who truly believes and lives according to his faith has become rare.

How many pious Christians are there? Only God knows. But judging from their actions, most Christians seem to be Christians in name only. I ask: Can a man be Christian and yet not pray? Can he go to bed and rise from it without prayer? Or sit down to eat, without feeling the need to cross himself? Can a man be a Christian and yet never open the Holy Bible to read a chapter and so nourish his soul with clear spiritual food? Can a man be a Christian and not attend church, never confess, never receive Holy Communion? Can a man be a Christian and yet use foul language, commit adultery, keep company with heretics? Can such a man be a Christian?

Today, a Christian Diogenes should walk the streets with his lantern, saying: "I'm looking for a Christian. An Orthodox Christian, pious and virtuous." For these Christians the Church prays: "For the pious and Orthodox Christians, let us pray to the Lord."

The pious and Orthodox Christians! Our Church prays for them! And the rest? Does the Church ignore them? Certainly not. Anyone who has been baptized in the name of the Holy Trinity, unless he denies Christ, remains a Christian. But such Christians are like sheep who have left the fold and are wandering into ravines and forests, in danger of being eaten by wolves, if they have not been eaten already. The pious priest, who has such Christians in his own parish, like the good shepherd, must seek out these sheep and save them from danger. He must work very hard. If other bad shepherds scatter the flock, he must work even harder to increase the fold, to increase church attendance and participation.

This priest will be a very happy man if, before he passes away, he can see the last sheep of his parish return to the holy fold of Orthodoxy. Then these people also will be included among those for whom we pray in the beautiful petition: "For the pious and Orthodox Christians, let us pray to the Lord."

FOR THE BISHOP

"For our Archbishop . . ., let us pray to the Lord."

This request is the fifth of the petitions which the Church addresses to God at the beginning of the Divine Liturgy. With this request the faithful are called to pray to God first for their Bishop, then for the presbyters and deacons, and last for all the clergy and the laity.

"For our Archbishop...." But who is the Archbishop, for whom we Christians must pray? Today, the Archbishop is called the first among the bishops of an Apostolic Church, such as the Church of Greece, of Cyprus, etc. But in the ancient Church, the Archbishop's responsibilities were the same as those of the present-day Metropolitan; that is, he was the administrator of a Church district. He was called Archbishop, not only because there were other bishops in the districts who depended on him, but also because in those days even the presbyters and the priests were sometimes called bishops. As St. Chrysostom says, the priest of the Most High differs only a little from the bishop. Except for the ordination and the consecration of a church, the priest has the same duties and rights as the bishop, but administers to a smaller district.

The bishop's role is necessary to the Church. The three epistles of the Apostle Paul addressed to the bishops, the administrators of Church districts, testifies to the need for such an office. But the office of the bishop must not be over-emphasized and made to be like a worldly power. The bishop is a brother in Christ. As the first among equals, he must behave towards the other priests as an older brother to his younger brothers.

The difference between the bishop and the priest is chiefly this: while the priest is responsible for only one parish, the bishop is responsible for all the Christians of his metropolitan district. For he cannot remain indifferent about anything that happens within his district. If the Church is called militant, because it is made up of Christians who have to fight the spiritual struggle, then the bishop should be thought of as a general, responsible for all the officers and soldiers, that is, the priests and laymen respectively.

But if we think of who directs this spiritual army in all times and places, then we realize that all of us – bishops, priests, deacons, and laymen – are only soldiers of Christ's army. Our Lord Jesus Christ is commander-in-chief. He is the administrator and the victor. He has defeated the devil and death. He Himself directs and governs His Church through His representatives, who are the bishops and the priests. In His name, the bishops and the priests govern the Church.

The bishop has an enormous responsibility. And as an imperfect and weak human being, he has many enemies who threaten him spiritually. The devil fights him. The devil's agents, the heretics and atheists, fight him. The "old man" within him, his former self – his past sins and vices – lives on and fights him. Every Christian is persecuted from these internal and external, visible and invisible enemies, but the bishop is persecuted more. The fall of the bishop will have a terrible impact. The faithful will lose their zeal, and those already weak in their faith will lose it altogether. The flock will disperse. The Lord described what would happen: "I will kill the shepherd and the sheep of the flock will be scattered" (Matt. 26:31).

If the shepherd is lost, the sheep likewise will be lost. That is why the devil rages against the bishop. And if the devil cannot corrupt the bishop, he does not admit defeat. He works to undermine the bishop's authority with the slanders and lies spread throughout the district. He even stirs up such hate in some men that they plot to murder the bishop, as Church history attests.

If the bishop were without authority and power, and was instead a simple layman, he would be loved and honored in his community where people would recognize his spiritual gifts. But because he wears the cassock of the clergy, and preaches, and chastises men (the high as well as low) for their sins, those who are far from God hate this man. They hate the bishop, the clergymen, the faithful and the victorious as they would have hated Christ, if they had lived in His age. They hate the light, for their works are of darkness. The unbelievers and the impious regard the bishop, who seriously tries to perform his duty as demanded in the Gospels, as the greatest obstacle to the satisfaction of their dark desires. Such a bishop must be done away with, by any means possible, so that evil and corrupt men can have their way.

"For our Archbishop..., let us pray to the Lord." The bishop who lives in this twentieth century, this age of unbelief and unimaginable corruption, is in danger from organized attacks of evil, and is in need of spiritual help. He must not fight this fight by himself, because his is a struggle which concerns us all, the strengthening of faith, the salvation of souls. All the faithful, all the honest friends of the good and the beautiful, must stay at the bishop's side and must like soldiers fight for the victory of the cross. The bishop must not fall. He must win, for his victory will be the victory of the Church, the victory of Orthodoxy.

Please do not think that I have said all this because I myself am a bishop and want you to support me. Whatever I have said, I have said for every bishop of the Orthodox Church, in every part of the world — for every bishop who, despite his human failings, believes in Christ and fights to spread the light of the Christian faith to others. Such a bishop is like a father. And as a father, he must be loved and supported by all his spiritual children. As much as the enemies of the faith hate him, so much his spiritual children love him.

For such a bishop, let the faithful kneel and pray continuously. By so doing, they carry out the Church's call: "For the Archbishop . . ., let us pray to the Lord."

CLERGY AND LAITY

"For . . . all the clergy and the laity, let us pray to the Lord."

We are here concerned, dear brothers in Christ, with the second part of the fifth petition addressed to our Triune God at the beginning of the Divine Liturgy. The first part of this petition, you will remember, called on the faithful to pray for the bishop of their district, the priests and the deacons. In this second part, the faithful are asked to pray for all the clergy and the laity.

Most people, when they think of the Church, think of the bishops and priests. Such a view of the Church is false. The Church, as we have said before, is made up of all those who believe in the Lord Jesus Christ, accept His divine teachings, and try to execute His commandments in their lives and to participate in the sacramental life.

The presbyters and deacons are servants of the people in their religious needs. They prepare the table on which the heavenly food — the most holy Body and precious Blood of our Lord Jesus Christ — is served, and they invite all Christians to partake of it. They serve the people not only in this sacrament of the Divine Eucharist, but also in all the other mysteries. And their service extends beyond the spiritual to the material, for they help to satisfy their people's material needs when such needs occur. In case of famine, for example, the clergymen do all they possibly can to save their people from starvation.

If the clergymen forget that they are the servants of the pious people, they are then in danger of becoming mere professionals who perform their holy duties routinely, for salaries and gifts, without regard for the material and spiritual needs of their people.

The Lord taught us, by word as well as by example, that the clergyman is the servant of the people. On Holy Thursday, at the Last Supper, Christ put on an apron, filled a basin with water, bent down, and washed His disciples' feet. The Apostle Peter was, however, strongly opposed to this. He thought it a humiliation for his Master. But Christ insisted, threatening to exclude Peter from the fellowship if he refused His service, and so Peter gave in. By this action Christ taught His disciples that their mission was to serve others. A true disciple must be motivated to act from a sincere love and profound humility. He must never act as a master or tyrant, but as a servant and loving father. "I gave you," said Christ, "an example. As I did, so must you do. And if you follow my example, you will be happy" (John 13:15-17).

The people must not be thought of as a flock of dumb animals, to whom the master can do whatever he wants — mistreat, sell, or even kill — but rather they must be thought of as rational and free human beings who, from the hour of their Baptism, have become children of God. The laymen, then, are precious members of the Church.

Priests and archpriests need a pious congregation in order to be understood. For this reason a priest or a bishop cannot be ordained to serve a community which has no Christians. There must be a parish or a Diocese;there must be souls, even if only a handful, to whom the clergyman can administer. For such souls the God-

Man, the good shepherd, was sacrificed. The laity are not slaves, but brothers-in-Christ of the clergyman, and like brothers they, too, have rights in the Church.

We read in the acts of the Apostles that, in the early years of the Church, the laity had certain rights; they voted, for instance, on Church matters. This is especially evident in the case of the traitor Judas' suicide. This unworthy disciple's death left a void in the fellowship which had to be filled. One might suspect that the Apostles together, or perhaps Peter himself, would choose Judas' successor. But instead the Apostles called together their fellow Christians, 120 men and women in all, and asked them to choose. These 120 people suggested two candidates, Justus and Matthias, and again the Apostles did not choose from between the two, but had them draw lots, and so finally admitted Matthias to their ranks (Acts 1:15-26).

The Apostles left the Church a legacy of election. The pious people of the first centuries gathered together to elect their bishops. The collective voice of these people was considered the voice of God. In this manner hierarchs were elected who glorified the Church with their luminous thought and holy lives.

Unfortunately, today the pious people are ignored. Today the bishops and the archbishops are elected by a synod of hierarchs. This, however, does not agree with the ancient practice of the Church. And it also does not serve the best interests of the Church. It is possible today for a hard-working clergyman, well-loved by the people of his province, to be ignored in the election of the bishop in favor of a man unknown in the area but skilled in flattering influential bishops and thereby winning their favor. Bishops are therefore no longer always virtuous men, but often insincere flatterers, the favorites of certain hierarchs. The people are ignored, not only in the election of bishops, but also of priests, and even parish councils.

The election system must change. We must re-establish the Apostolic practice of election. Clergy and laity must elect and the bishops must ordain.

But we must stress that in order for such an electoral system to work, the list of eligible voters among the laity must be purged of those who publicly live un-Christian lives. Unbelievers, atheists, blasphemers, and scandal-mongers must not be allowed to vote. Only then is there hope that there will once again dawn an ecclesiastic renaissance.

THE NATION

"For our pious nation . . ., let us pray to the Lord."

Let us continue, beloved, to talk about the great supplication. The great supplication is a series of petitions. The petition which we will try to explain is the sixth one, which contains two separate requests. In it we pray to God for two things. The first is for our nation, the second for our army. In this homily we will consider the first, our nation.

O Lord, protect and guard our nation! But what is a nation? This world is not composed of one nation, but of many nations. Granted, during the last few years, all nations have decided to have a measure of unity, at least externally, and they have formed a big international organization, which is called the United Nations (U.N.).

But nations still differ from each other. How are they different? They are like men. All men have many similarities and characteristics in common, although they certainly demonstrate their individual differences. This is how we distinguish one person from another person, and we recognize him by his distinct personality. This same thing is true with nations. They have many similarities between them, but the differences in ways of life, manners, and customs are very apparent. And seeing these differences, we are able to distinguish one nation from another. Each nation has its own character.

The question arises, what is it which differentiates one nation from another? The land? The mountains and plains? The rivers, the lakes, and the seas? Certainly, these are factors. But these are not the chief characteristics, because it is possible for the people of a nation to loose their country, to be dispersed to the four corners of the earth, and still remain conscious that they belong to their own nation. To some of them, this consciousness is so strong that even after the passage of centuries, their descendants continue to relate to the idea of their nationhood.

Is it perhaps the language that is the distinctive mark of a nation? The language is one of the differentiating characteristics. Yes, language is a mark, but not always the main sign. Because history testifies to the fact that there have been men who once spoke the same language, and, due to various reasons, lost their ancestral language, learned other languages, even the language of their conquerors, and in spite of this, did not loose their national consciousness. The Greeks of Asia Minor and Macedonia are examples of this. In Asia Minor many Greeks lived in the remote areas of Turkey. They lost their ancestral language and spoke Turkish, and during this same time, while they themselves spoke in Turkish, they were cognizant of the fact that they were Greeks, and upon hearing the word Greece, would be moved to tears. They were Turks in their language but Greeks in their heart. This same thing happened to Greeks living in parts of Macedonia. Some of them forgot Greek and learned to speak a local language, the so-called Macedonian. This did not mean that they forgot their nation. When the need arose, they fought and sacrificed themselves for Greece. While speaking Slavic, they thought Greek. A foreign language, yes, but with a Greek heart.

But hovering above the soil, the rivers, the seas, above the monuments of antiquity, above the language, above the customs, and traditions of our nation, is the most important mark, our faith, the Orthodox faith. It is the Orthodox faith that connects and unites us. This is all too evident in the Greeks of the diaspora. Three million Greeks are scattered in foreign countries. What is it which binds them and does not let them forget the motherland? It is the Church. More specifically, all those churches which were built by the sweat of the immigrants, in all of those far-flung places. In these churches, they congregate every Sunday and on the great holy days, attend the Divine Liturgy, and remember the motherland. It is a fact that those immigrants who were influenced by various anti-nation and anti-Christian propagandas and left the Orthodox Church, lost, along with their faith, their national consciousness. They became internationalists, a people without a motherland, and they speak with contempt about the Greek nation.

Now, someone might say, by the way you are speaking, you are telling us to love only our own nation, and to hate other nations. Not so. That would be misinterpreting us. We do not say that one should hate other nations, because all nations, according to Christian teaching, have a divine origin. St. Paul preached this very clearly while standing on the most important platform of the pagan world, the Acropolis. There he stood in front of our ancestors who scorned the other nations, calling them barbarians, and preached that all nations have their place under the sun. God made the boundaries of every nation. The Father of all nations is God. And if even a small sparrow does not fall dead without the will of the heavenly Father, then a nation cannot fall, be destroyed, and disappear without God's will.

God wants all nations to live with justice, love and harmony. But unfortunately, the nations do not want to live as God wants them to. There were, there are, and there will be nations which, like wild beasts, rush out of their cages to attack smaller and weaker ones, and want to tear them to pieces. And thus, the small nations are endangered by the larger and stronger ones, as well as by stronger regimes.

Our motherland, Greece, is a small nation. Yes, it is a small nation! But, it is an historic and glorious one. We do not just say this, reality shouts it. It cultivated letters, the arts and sciences, and offered to humanity more than any other nation.

But this small nation was also persecuted in the past by big and powerful nations, by barbarian people who wanted to annihilate it. They wanted this lamp, which burns and illuminates through the ages, and is called Greece, to be extinguished. But it could not be done. Even now, Greece is in danger from barbarians from the East. They want its sea, they want its islands, they want it all.

For this reason, we who go to church, must raise our hands to heaven and pray to God for this martyred country. "For our pious nation..., let us pray to the Lord."

THE CHRIST-LOVING ARMY

"For our Christ-loving army, on land, air, and sea, let us pray to the Lord."

Now we will explain the second part of the sixth petition in the great supplication. It is an ardent plea for our army, navy, and air force.

There are those who object to this petition. They are so-called men of "peace." They are hypocrites. They cry out for peace, but they do not love it. They accuse the Church, in its prayers for the army, of opposing Christ. Christ's birth in this world was heralded by the angelic hymn of peace. Christ preached peace. He blessed the peacemakers. Christ told the Apostle Peter at Gethsemane, when he pulled out his knife and cut off the ear of Malchos, the archpriest's servant, to put the knife back in its case. And lastly, the first word Christ said when He arose from the grave was "peace." "Peace be unto you" (John 20:19). The Church continuously repeats this word in the Divine Liturgy. It starts with peace: "In peace let us pray to the Lord." How, they ask, can we now pray that the army defeat and subdue "under its feet, every hostile enemy?" We have compromised ourselves, they say, by asking for two opposing requests in the same series of petitions.

The Church, beloved, continues Christ's preaching, the preaching of peace. She preaches that if men will believe in Christ, peace will prevail all over the world.

Unfortunately, however, as you well know, most people do not want to believe in Christ. They do not want to live according to His divine commandments. They live according to their own evil designs; they deceive, they steal, do wrong, commit hosts of crimes, and, because of this sinfulness of mankind, fights and wars break out.

Christ continues to offer peace to the world through the voice of the Church. But the world does not accept this peace, and even mocks it. Who then, is responsible, if this peace does not prevail in the world? Men, who do not love Christ's peace, but love the ways of this life, which inherently leads to fratricide. Wars are the whips of a sinful mankind.

Very well, some might say! But what are the army and the weapons needed for?

I will give you an example. St. John Chrysostom mentioned it first. Let us assume that a preacher goes to a place where a thousand people are living. He preaches about thievery. He interprets God's commandment: "Do not steal" (Exod. 20:14). He develops his theme well, he gives examples and arguments, and trys to convince them just how evil a thing stealing really is. Most of the listeners are convinced. Some, however, are not. They insist on stealing. They even say it publicly. It is their way of life. "Snatch to eat, and steal to have." Thus, with this contradiction the situation changes. What must be done? Will the majority let the few steal and do whatever they want, or will they take measures to prevent this evil? Naturally, they will choose the second. Those who do not want to obey God's law, "You shall not steal", will be forced to obey the authority which the community has designated. And this authority is not without weapons. For the evil-doers, it has the sword.

St. Chrysostom said: I hold a cross and I tell you: "You shall not steal", "You shall not kill", but you do not want to listen to me. Therefore, let the authority of the state, governed by laws, arrest you. For the commandments: "You shall not steal", "You shall not kill", are written on the swords of the Christian authorities.

The Apostle Paul also preached the same thing when he said that this type of an authority is God's servant; it supports the work of God's kingdom; it praises good and punishes evil (Rom 13:3-7).

The army, then, is the sword of authority. It is necessary. Abolish the army, abolish every armed force, and immediately a terrible monster appears, tears everything to pieces, and makes life unbearable. What is the name of this monster? Anarchy. All the evil-doing elements — the thieves, the murderers, the deceivers, and the exploiters — will prevail, and no one will be able to stop them.

The army is then necessary. It will be necessary until the day comes when all men believe in Christ and subject themselves to the Holy Gospel. Until then, the Churches will pray for the army.

"For our Christ-loving army, on land, air, and sea, let us pray to the Lord." But the army is necessary, not only for order and security inside the state, but also for the protection of the borders of the country, for defense and protection against foreign enemies. Criminal elements exist outside of the nation also. They are the "barbarous nations, wanting wars." For there are powerful states which make wars to extend their boundaries over into others, and try to dominate the entire world. And when a state makes war in order to destroy the freedom and independence of a small nation, this state becomes like a pack of wolves ready to rush upon a flock of sheep. What should the shepherd do? Open the door to the wolves and say to them: "Please come in...?" The good shepherd will never do this. He will set the sheep-dogs to bark and chase the wolves, and he himself will chase them with stones and slings. A nation does the same thing when a barbarous state attacks and wants to conquer it. It fights the invaders.

All those who pretend that they want peace, and ask that the army be abolished, remind us of one of Aesop's fables. The wolves went to a shepherd and proposed peace, but, under one condition: the shepherd should get rid of the sheepdogs. But the shepherd understood their cunning purpose. They wanted the sheepfold unguarded so that they could enter it easily and destroy the sheep. The so-called peacemakers act the same way. They shout: "Down with the weapons, down with the army, so that the nation will be unguarded, and its enemies can do to it whatever they want." The Christians, who love their nation, love also its guardians. They pray to God for them.

WHO SAVES THE CITIES

"For this city and for this community, for every city and country, and for the faithful who dwell therein, let us pray to the Lord."

This is the seventh petition in the great supplication.

Man is not self-sufficient: he cannot live alone. He is a social creature who feels the need to live with others. As a result, he has built villages and cities. Cities in our days have evolved into megalopolises, having populations exceeding that of the entire nation of Greece, coming close to, or even surpassing ten million.

Being Christians, we should pray to God for the city or village in which we live. This demands our concern. The happiness of others is our happiness, too. Unfortunately, few understand this and pray to God for the whole. Most people pray only for themselves, their spouses, and children: beyond themselves and their families, they pray for no one else.

But this is called selfishness, and selfishness is a sin that grows little by little, and spreads, becoming the root of all evils.

Let us mention an instructive story. We all know that Rome was the largest city in the ancient world. At one time, Rome was invaded, sacked, and burned. When the news arrived in another city, the people were upset, and discussed the matter. One woman, however, started crying. "How compassoinate a woman," said the others.

But this woman was not crying for a city called Rome, she was crying for a chicken she had, which she called Rome. When she heard the name Rome, she thought for her chicken. But when she learned that it was not her chicken that was lost, but the city of Rome, she stopped crying. Imagine! She cried for a chicken, and not for a city of a million people.

Most people do this. They grieve for their own calamities, but they do not grieve – they do not even care – for the misfortunes of other people. Let the whole world go up in flames, as long as nothing happens to them.

Something like this happened to the prophet Jonah. He felt sorry for a squash plant which dried up and died, but he did not grieve for a whole city (Jonah 4:5-11).

Our Church condemns selfishness, even under the religious mantle by which we think we shall save our own souls. Our Church calls us to pray for "this city or town...." By these words we are commanded to pray for all the Christians, all the inhabitants, wherever they may live.

Yes, someone might say, we should pray for the cities and the villages. But what can my prayer do for the welfare and protection of a city or village?

What can it do? If you open the Holy Bible, you will find passages and examples that show the great help the prayers of people can bring towards the salvation of a city, or even a whole nation. We are reminded of Abraham. This faithful servant of God was living in a very corrupt age. God decided to destroy two degenerate cities of ancient idolatry, Sodom and Gomorrah, by fire. But first, He told Abraham. Abraham, upon hearing

God's decision, was horrified, and he asked Him: "If I find 50, 45, 40, 30, 20, 10, righteous men, will You still destroy these cities? "No," answers God, "If only ten righteous men are found, for those ten I will spare them..." (Gen. 18:24-32). But unfortunately, in these two cities, not even ten righteous ones could be found, and the cities were destroyed, except the righteous Lot and the members of his family.

Therefore, according to the Scriptures, the saviors of the cities are the righteous and the saints. The destroyers are the sinners, the unrepentant people who, inspite of all the invitations of God, still refuse to acknowledge their sins. And because of the sins and crimes of the inhabitants, villages, cities, and even great states were destroyed.

At one time a terrible earthquake shook Constantinople, and supplications and litanies were offered. St. John Chrysostom preached and said that the cause of the earthquake was the sins of the inhabitants, and worst of all, the avarice and greed of the rich.

Saints save the world. Unrepentant sinners destroy it.

All of us, clergy and laity, with pain and with tears in our eyes, must confess that in our own century sins have multiplied terribly. Even in small villages people sin by committing crimes, known and unknown, which never used to happen. But the people who live in the cities sin much more, because there the means of corruption are greater, and evil and crime hardly come to light.

The angels, who are appointed by God to watch over every city, town, village, groan over our many sins. Only we sinful and criminal people do not groan over them. We do not realize that our sins are contributing to the coming destruction. Yes! According to the words of the Holy Bible, villages and cities, people and nations, great and powerful states, will be destroyed, as Sodom and Gomorrah were destroyed in the ancient world. They will be destroyed because of the sins of the people who live in them.

Calamities will be prevented, or the days of great sorrow will be shortened, if righteous ones are found in every town and city, people who are actual saints, who truly believe in Christ and live the commandments of the Bible. These righteous people will save the world from calamity.

For this reason, the Church calls on its believers to pray with faith to God "for this city...., and that this city and every city and country may be spared from famine and pestilence, earthquake and flood, fire and sword, foreign invasion and civil war, and sudden death; that God may divert from us all threatening danger and disease, and save us from His just anger that hangs over us; and that He may have mercy on us."

CHRIST BLESSES

"For seasonable weather, for the abundance of the fruits of the earth, and for peaceful times, let us pray to the Lord."

There are many people who criticize Christianity in our times. They say that it does not concern itself with the basic needs of mankind, which are food, clothing, shelter, etc.; Christianity cares only for the soul and for paradise, as if man is only a spirit and not a body also. This kind of Christianity, its enemies say, we don't need. We will let it build castles in the air, while we will turn to other systems that promise us bread, clothes, houses, and whatever else we need for our earthly happiness.

But this accusation against Christianity is unjust. Pure Christianity, as was preached by its founder, the God-Man, taught by the Church Fathers, and practiced by true Christians not only with words but with deeds, does not ignore the material needs of man. Christ did not preach war against the body and its physical needs; neither did He ignore them. He showed His concern even by performing miracles. In His first miracle at the wedding of Cana, He showed His concern for the need that occurred. At this wedding, as you know, the wine ran out and the bridegroom became distressed. Christ was not indifferent, He ordered that the empty jars be filled with water, He blessed them, and the water was immediately changed to wine. And yes, into fine quality wine, better than the one they had consumed before.

Also, in another case, when there were thousands of people – men, women, and children – with Him in the desert with nothing to eat, Christ did not show indifference, He fed all the people. He blessed five loaves of bread and two fish, and the miracle happened; the few provisions were multiplied, and there was enough for all those thousands of people to eat. This miracle was in agreement with the prayer: "Our Father...," which He taught us to say (Matt. 6:9-13). In this short prayer, which the faithful address to the heavenly Father, there is a request to preserve the human body: "Give us this day our daily bread." We ask the heavenly Father to give us the food we need every day.

Christ, therefore, the founder of our religion, was not indifferent to our needs. And our Church, which continues Christ's work on earth, does not ignore them either. And if there are representatives of the faith who are indifferent to the people, and do not care if they are hungry and suffering, it would not be right to charge it against Christianity, or to judge and condemn it for the behavior of those unworthy representatives of the Crucified One. There were, and there always will be, Judases, traitors, and exploiters of Christianity.

The Divine Liturgy is one of the proofs that our Church does not ignore the material and bodily needs of humanity. In it there are not only prayers for the spiritual needs of man, but also for his material needs. Consider the eighth petition of the great supplication, as you read it at the beginning of this homily. To repeat: "For seasonable weather, for the abundance of the fruits of the earth, and for peaceful times, let us pray to the Lord."

In this petition, we ask the heavenly Father for three things. First, seasonable weather. Second, the abundance of the fruits of the earth. And third, peaceful times. Let us examine in detail the contents of this petition.

First, we ask for "seasonable weather." What is "seasonable weather?" For the weather to be beneficial and useful to agriculture, it must be neither very cold nor very hot. If the weather is very cold and the temperature goes below freezing, then the fruit-bearing trees suffer greatly. And if the cold gets worse, then the sap of the trees freezes and the trees are frost-burned by the ice. On the other hand, if the weather becomes very hot, as when the wind which comes from the Sahara and is called "siroco" blows, then whole plains which are green with crops dry and burn, and rich harvests are destroyed. And if it is stormy and tempestuous, with the wind blowing too strongly, it is catastrophic to agriculture. It flattens the crops, destroys orchards, uproots small and large trees, and leaves the earth looking as if a wild battle had taken place on it.

But who commands the air? They say that it is a natural phenomenon. Yes, it is. But who governs this? Who created the air which, as we know, contains one of the most beneficial and useful elements, oxygen? Air does not exist on the moon and on the other planets. Lack of air means lack of life. Without suitable air, clean from various germs and other micro-organisms, who can live? The air which blows over the earth is a creation of the all good and powerful God, and for that reason, we ask Him for air which is proper for agriculture and, in general, for our whole life.

O God, give us healthy and clean air!

When seasonable weather exists, then an abundance of the fruits of the earth also exists. The industriousness of man and the knowledge of true agricultural science which bring progress to farming, certainly contribute much to the abundance of the earth. But we must not forget that the most important contribution is God's blessing. Let our farmers labor as much as they want. Let them fertilize the earth with the best fertilizers. Let them plant the fields with the best seed. Let them cultivate the land in the best way. Let them spray the trees with insecticides. If Christ does not bless and the clouds do not bring rain, and a beneficial wind does not blow, and the sun does not warm the seeds, all the labors and all the concerns of science are in vain. Countries with endless rich lands, which could feed not only their own people but others, could go hungry and suffer if the blessing of God is lacking. But on the other hand, poor countries, small in size, if together with the people's love of work, have God's blessings, then these poor and small nations see the miracle of God, become self-sufficient in the most important crops, and in some cases even export wheat and other provisions to richer nations. And here we see how true is the word of God. "Rich men have turned poor and gone hungry; but they that seek the Lord shall not be deprived of any good things" (Psalm 33:11).

So far, we have explained two requests. The third one remains: "Permit, O Lord, that we may have peaceful times." But what are these peaceful times, and what relationship do they have with harvesting of the fruits of the earth? Peaceful times are when in the relations between nations, peace prevails, there are no wars, and no threats of war are heard to keep the people in anxiety. When fear of war exists, the farmers hesitate to cultivate the earth and thus the production of agriculture falls.

We, the Greek people, have bitter experience of wartime. Let us remember August and September of 1922. In Asia Minor and Pontus, the Christians had harvested their crops and were getting ready for winter. But suddenly, the great disaster struck. The war front broke and the Greeks fled to save themselves, leaving everything behind. All of the rich harvest of that summer was lost. The Greek population then went hungry and suffered, especially the refugees. Let us also remember the years of the occupation. The Germans used to feed their horses with select grain while the suffering people had none. A half- million people died from hunger.

These two examples show how important peaceful times are for agriculture and the happiness of a country. Even the richest country hungers and suffers in time of war. Others sow, and others harvest. Barbarous peoples, like thieves, rob the wealth of the conquered and condemn then to hunger and annihilation. For this reason the Church exhorts the faithful to pray to God to give "peaceful times."

THOSE WHO ARE TRAVELLING

"For those who travel by water and by land, for the sick, for the afflicted, for captives, and for their salvation, let us pray to the Lord."

This is the ninth request in the series of petitions of the great supplication.

When the Church prays, she does not remember only the farmers. Being an affectionate mother, she remembers all her children. And with this ninth petition, she calls us to pray "for those who travel by water and by land, for the sick, for the afflicted, for the captives, and for their salvation." With this prayer, it is as if our Church is addressing everyone in the congregation and saying:

"You my Christians, who at this moment find yourself inside the church and are following the Divine Liturgy, think of how many people find themselves outside of the church, not because they do not want to come, but because they are in various difficult and dangerous situations. Think, that at this moment, somewhere on the sea, vessels are travelling with thousands of passengers and some of them may be in danger of sinking by the angry waves of a storm. Even if you find yourself far away, you may greatly help those who travel on the sea. By your warm prayer "for those who travel," you may save people."

"Think also, that there are people who are travelling on land, and they are in greater danger today than in former times. Then, they were in danger from robbers and wild animals. Today's people, who travel by cars are in greater danger. All the roads have been painted with the blood of people who are killed every day in automobile accidents. And most of them happen on Sunday.*"

"But besides those travelling on sea and on land, in our days there are also those travelling by air. They are in danger from airplane accidents. Our petition must include them, too."

"Think again that there are thousands of sick people in hospitals and clinics, who are in pain, and suffering, and there is not a soul to comfort them. Think that at this time there is someone who is very sick, he is fighting with death, and from moment to moment his soul might leave his tortured body and travel to the other world."

"Think also of those men who are working at difficult jobs in unhealthy conditions, in coal mines and other mines, and their lives are in danger. Pray for them, too, those hidden heroes, who work and labor for the entire community."

"Think as well about other people — people who are not free to move and go wherever they please, because cruel tyrants captured them and put them in prison."

"Think, my Christian, while you are attending the Liturgy, about all those whom we have mentioned, and say a prayer to God for them. This prayer is a duty which must be performed by everyone who is attending Liturgy. But the Christian must not only restrict himself to prayers, he must also do whatever he can for them.

A visit to the hospital, or to the prison, a little help, a letter, or whatever else you can offer to your brothers in danger, is the fulfillment of the great commandment of love, which must be expressed by all means."

Let us pray to God for those who travel by water, by land, and by air, for the sick, the afflicted, and the captives. Let us pray, the petition adds, for their salvation as well. That means that we must ask God not only to save them from bodily danger, but more importantly, for the salvation of their immortal souls. We must pray that their souls be strengthened by divine grace, that they do not become timid and lose courage, but heroically confront the pains and difficulties of life, and become worthy of divine blessedness: "Blessed is the man that endureth temptation: for when he is tried, he shall receive the crown of life" (James 1:12).

A certain contemporary saint says that when we hear the petition "for those who travel...", we should be moved by the very thought that thousands and millions of our fellow men suffer and are in danger every moment. But where is this holy emotion today? Most of us hear this moving petition of the Church coldly and indifferently. Alas! Selfishness has deadened inside us the feeling of Christian love, that love which stretches out and embraces the entire world.

*Sunday starts on Saturday evening at sunset, according to the ancient tradition of the Hebrews, and according to the Orthodox Church as well. Thus, the petition includes that most dangerous part of the week for travellers.

LAKE OF TEARS

"For our deliverance from all tribulation, wrath, danger and necessity, let us pray to the Lord."

The Church, beloved, is the affectionate mother who remembers all her children, and cares for them. In our previous petition we have seen her praying for "those who travel by water and land, for the sick, for the afflicted, for captives, and for their salvation." Now in the tenth petition, the Church extends the wings of her love further and embraces even more people, who are experiencing other kinds of difficulties and sorrows in this world, and this does not mean that these sorrows cannot be heavier than the previous ones.

Let us give an example. Some time ago, a young man came to the offices of the diocese. He was married not long ago. He married a young woman whom he loved, and he hoped that he would be happy with her. But unfortunately, this young woman, who before the marriage appeared like an angel in his eyes, after the wedding, unmasked evils and vices. The young man, now deeply upset and grief-stricken over the marriage, had reached the point of asking for a divorce. I invited the young lady as well, and tried to reconcile them. But the young man was adamant: "I cannot live with her anymore," he said, "she has made my life miserable; I'd rather be jailed than bring her back home again."

You see, my beloved, that not only those who are jailed suffer inside their darkened cells. There are other kinds of prisoners who, even though they are free, taste worse sorrows. Yes. There are men suffering because of their wives. They suffer from their caprices, from their tongues, which sting them every day.

But there are also women, honorable and good homemakers, who suffer from their husbands, who are drinkers, drunkards, gamblers, come home after midnight to curse and abuse them, and make their homes a hell. Women who have such husbands are like those women who, during the years of persecution, suffered martyrdom by the enemies of Christianity. These women have a life-long martyrdom.

There are fathers and mothers who experience many sorrows from their children, who do not obey or respect them, but curse their parents with vulgar words and even raise a hand to hit them. How many of these parents do not bend under the weight of sorrow, do not lose their joy and their health, and do not die embittered! But also there are children suffering from the cruelty, the unbelief and impiety of their parents; parents who become angry, swear and blaspheme them when they see that they are children of the Church. Such parents are like St. Barbara's father.

Oh, how many sorrows man experiences in the midst of his family! How many tears are being shed every day from the eyes of spouses, parents, children! From the place where someone is expecting comfort and support, he tastes distress and sorrows. And thus Christ's word is true: "And a man's foes shall be those of his own household" (Matt. 10:36).

A person experiences sorrows and distresses outside of the family as well, coming from other people with whom he is obliged to have various relationships. Seldom are the relationships with other people smooth, peaceful, and pleasant. Conflicts take place every day. Employees suffer when they are under the authority of unjust supervisors, who are not of a mind to appreciate their labor. Workers suffer and groan under the bad behavior of those directing businesses. Others who want to work in their own hometowns and start a family, cannot find work, and with tears in their eyes, are forced to go abroad to far countries, and to work very hard to earn their living. And others who put their trust in men and invest in corporations and trusts, become victims of deceivers and exploiters; with their savings they helped others to become rich, and now they are lacking even their daily bread. I know a man who came from America, who brought much money, helped relatives and friends, and in the end was abandoned by them. He was forced to seek shelter in a home for the aged. He is distressed and grieved. No one visits him anymore. He is alone, deserted and abandoned. How many old people like him spend the last moments of their lives inside homes for the aged!

But who can describe all the sorrows of mankind? There are sorrows which are visible, and there are sorrows which are not. And these sorrows which someone holds secretly inside his heart and does not tell anyone are the greatest sorrows of the world. If someone could collect the tears which are shed and are still being shed by people in the whole world, that person would be able to make a great lake, a bitter lake, a lake which should be named: "The Lake of Human Sorrows."

But besides these sorrows, which come from the family and the community, which are not consistent with God's will, there are other sorrows which come as a scourging, a punishment for the sins and crimes of mankind. What are these sorrows?

A horrible storm sweeps the sea and sinks ships. A river floods and destroys a whole plain. An earthquake buries hundreds and thousands of people under ruins. A volcano erupts and a river spreads death to millions of people. Great afflictions, coming from the elements of nature against sinful mankind, are, according to Scripture, an expression of divine anger. The Lord foretold this: "Great tribulation will come which never before happened in the world. Great and terrible signs will occur. There shall be great earthquakes and famines and sickness and horrible things and great signs from heaven" (Matt. 24).

Oh! The anger of God is frightening. And the cause of God's anger are the sins of all. St. Cosmas Aitolos, in his teachings, used to say with tears and sighs, that because of our sins, God's anger fell on us and we are being punished. But we are not conscious of it, and continue to sin. Let us pay attention, the holy man of God used to say, for if we continue to sin and do not repent, then woe to mankind. With as much ease as a stick breaks clay vessels, God will shatter sinful mankind, which, instead of life, prefers sin, death, and destruction.

For this reason, my beloved, in these fearful days, we must hear the petition of the Church with deep emotion and pray "for our deliverance from all tribulation, wrath, danger, and necessity."

O MY SOUL, EMBRACE THE CROSS OF THE LORD

"Help, save, comfort and protect us, O God, by Thy grace."

This is the final request in the series of petitions in the great supplication. The present sermon will be devoted to it. When we understand what it means, we will no longer hear it coldly and indifferently, but instead, our prayer will ascend, warmed by our holy emotions, to the most gracious and almighty God.

Today, man thinks he is an omnipotent being. He has achieved things which previous generations only dreamed of. He went to the moon, and is trying to fly to other planets. Arrogantly successful, he despises the faith of simple people, and looking towards heaven, says: "God, I don't need you anymore. God is science, God is man!"

However, inspite of astonishing inventions and discoveries, he does not cease to be a weak creature. Some of his works may be preserved for centuries, like the pyramids of Egypt and the Parthenon of Athens. But man, who creates these works; if we may judge him physically, what is he? He is like a flower which today appears fresh and lustrous, but tomorrow withers and dries up. All it takes is one artery of the heart to break, one drop of blood to burst into the brain, and man will have a heart attack, a stroke, and he will die in a few minutes. Or man, who conquered the wild beasts and subjugated nature, is conquered by a tiny germ which cannot be seen by the naked eye, but by a microscope. And the interesting thing is this: that as much as the medicines increase, in the same proportion illnesses multiply. One of these diseases, the fearful illness of cancer, literally reaps humanity.

Man is sick and weak in body. But where he is much weaker is in the area of the soul, the area of moral and spiritual life. It is the evil which exists in the world of his soul. It is vices and evils. It is sin. Yes, sin, as we had the opportunity to speak about previously, is the most terrible germ which exists in the world. It enters into the soul as a deceitful thought, to which man pays no attention. But this evil thought, if it remains in the soul, can infect and poison the whole soul of man, and man will become a slave and a prisoner of sin. Science can kill the microbes of the body, but as for the germs which spoil and destroy the soul, who will be able to destroy and annihilate them? Man appears very sick and weak in this area of the soul's health.

While man, therefore, is in danger physically, he is in even greater danger in the area of his soul. And he is in need of God's help. But how many feel the need of help for their souls? Unfortunately, those who are conscious of the soul's danger are very few. Most are conscious only of bodily pains and dangers, and ask God's help. But for the spiritual danger, for the loss of the soul, not even a word. Only the body is to be saved.

We are reminded of the example of the two thieves who were crucified with Christ. Both suffered bodily. And they knew that in a few hours, they would no longer be alive. The one who was at Christ's left side, saw only approaching death, and because of this, together with people there, said to Christ: "If thou art the son of God, do thy miracle, come down from the cross and save us from this terrible death" (Matt. 27:40; Luke 23:39). The other thief, however, at the right hand of Christ, saw very far; he saw that beyond the danger which was threatening his body existed danger to his soul. These two men were sinful thieves. They had committed many crimes. Their hands were covered with blood – what would happen to their souls? The thought that he was a sinner and the thought of the other life beyond the grave, shocked the thief on the right. And at the last moment, this thief believed in Christ as savior of the world, and asked from Him forgiveness for his sins and the salvation of his soul. He asked this with a prayer, which is seldom addressed to God with such warmth: "Lord, remember me when Thou comest into Thy kingdom!" And Christ assured him that the salvation of his soul was secured. "Verily I say unto thee, today shalt thou be with me in paradise" (Luke 23:42- 43).

This thief was saved. This man, who was in danger of being submerged in the abyss of hell and losing his soul, at the last moment believed in the Crucified One, accepted His grace, and the cross of Christ became for his endangered soul the means of its salvation.

From that moment, the Lord's cross, not simply the wood, but the sacrifice which Christ offered on the cross, continues to be the inexhaustible fountain of our salvation. How can I express myself in order that you will understand this great truth of our faith? Let us assume that you are on a ship together with other passengers. Suddenly the ship, in the midst of a storm, plows into a rock and starts to sink. All the passengers fall into the sea. The waves are so wild that all are in danger of drowning. Suddenly another ship comes and the sailors throw lifebelts into the troubled sea. The shipwrecked persons able to grasp lifebelts are saved. Can you imagine with how much eagerness every person will grasp a lifebelt? In the same way, my beloved, all of us are shipwrecked sinners. We went astray and fell into the wild sea of sin. We are all in danger of being drowned in the black waves of hell. Only one will save us. The Crucified One, the Redeemer of the world, will save us.

From the height of the cross, He stretches His hand and wants to save us. He offers His almighty hand. Let us accept it. Let us offer our own hand, too. Our faith in the endless love of Christ, who condescended to be crucified for us, will be the means of our salvation. It will be as the lifebelt to the shipwrecked person.

O crucified Redeemer of the world! I, too, am a shipwrecked person who is in danger of being submerged and drowned in the black sea of sin. I embrace Thy cross, I hold it tightly with faith, and together with the others who are praying in the church, I direct to Thee, O Savior, my prayer and say: "Help, save, comfort and protect us, O God, by Thy grace."

THE SAINTS

"Commemorating our most holy, pure, blessed and glorified Lady, Theotokos and Ever-Virgin Mary, with all the Saints, let us commend ourselves and one another and our whole life to Christ, our God."

We have now come to the end of the great supplication. There were eleven petitions. We prayed to God for our material and our spiritual needs. We prayed for those living on earth. But are they the only ones who exist? Certainly not. There are also those who are not visible, the departed ones. This great multitude, which surpasses the number of those living on earth, includes all those who lived here on earth with faith in Christ and obeyed His sacred commandments. This is the triumphant Church, and its children are all the saints.

Now that the great supplication is ending, the priest exhorts the whole congregation to turn the attention of their souls to heaven. He calls on the Christians to remember all the saints, of which first among all of them, higher than even the angels and archangels, is the most holy Theotokos.

But before we speak about the mediation of the most holy Mother of God and of the saints, let us first answer the question as to who is called a saint. The word "saint" refers to a person clean of sin. But who in this world, I ask you, born in the natural way according to the law of sin, is pure? Pure is that which does not contain other substances. It is something rare even in the natural world. Let us take as an example gold, which is considered the most precious of metals. Does gold come from the depths of the earth pure? Certainly not. It is mixed with other, non-valuable elements. If it stays that way, its value is small. It must be cleaned. It must be separated from all the other worthless elements. For this, labor, skill and science are needed. The unclean masses of gold are brought into special ovens of high temperature, and there all the worthless elements which are mixed with the gold are burned out, or separated by fire, so that what remains is pure gold. Gold is purified by fire. And the curious thing is that the more times it goes through the oven, the more it is purified.

As gold does not come pure from the depths of the earth, so also man does not come pure from the maternal womb. Man tumbles from his mother's womb unclean, even bodily. He is a piece of flesh, covered with mucus, and if the natural instinct of motherhood did not exist, who would have the patience and courage to take care of the infant, as it is when it comes from the womb? Take away motherly affection, and you will see that infants cannot live without it. And unfortunately, we are living in an age when this natural affection of the mother towards the child is getting cool, and infants, who are born by mistake, are abandoned and are usually brought to orphanages.

Man is unclean. Unclean bodily. But what is bodily uncleanliness in comparison to the spiritual uncleanliness of man? Oh! If he could only see the dirt on his soul with which he is born, as he can see the bodily dirt, he would be both disgusted and terrified.

Man's soul is not like pure gold. It is like the gold which is mixed with various elements when it comes out of the earth. Man has inside himself much rust, and seeds of evil: a burdening inheritance from near and distant progenitors. It is that which, in the language of our Church, is called "ancestral sin". Science wants to present it somehow differently, and calls it bad heredity. It is, certainly, something mysterious. Nevertheless, it does not cease to be one of the greatest realities, and whoever forgets this cannot understand man. For this reason all mere human means for men's correction and regeneration fail.

Man's soul is unclean. Who can question this? And even if he lives only one day in this world, it is impossible for man to be free from the filth of sin.

No one, therefore, is clean. But how can someone be cleaned? How will someone become a saint? This for unaided mankind is impossible. To succeed, man needs divine help. But this purification of the human soul from evil, which like rust eats up whatever is pure and noble in the soul of man, does not work in a violent way. Man is not like the dead metal that the craftsman takes up, throws into the oven, and purifies. Man was created free, and must be willing to be cleansed, to be released from evil, from sin, and become a saint. But in order to be willing to reach saintliness, which is the source of true joy and happiness, man must become conscious of, and see, his sinful situation.

When someone considers himself healthy in body, he never goes to the doctor. But if he feels sick, he runs to him and asks to be cured. Something like this should happen with the one who is sick in soul, the sinner. A man who is a sinner — and who isn't a sinner? —

and is an egotist, thinking he is the best of people, will never become alarmed over his situation and ask for a spiritual doctor; whereas one who is humble, conscious of what a miserable state he is in, will ask for such a doctor. And the physician not only of the body, but most of all of the soul, is Christ. Without Christ's power it is impossible for man to be cleansed from internal evil.

Yes. Christ, with the mystery of holy Baptism, cleans the soul of ancestral sin, and also of other sins, personal sins, if the baptism takes place in adult age. And the soul of man becomes like the gold which comes from the oven, shining and glittering in its purity.

But the Christian who has been baptized must strive during his whole life to defeat sin and keep his soul pure from the stain of it. Is is possible? "The things which are impossible with men are possible with God" (Luke 18:27). The faithful, with God's help, fight the hard fight against sin and the "world," and inspite of all failures, finally conquer evil. And like a brave athlete, the faithful enter into the Kingdom of Heaven, into the triumphant Church. For without sanctification, no one can see the glory of God (Hebr. 12:14).

WAR AGAINST SAINTS

"Commemorating . . . with all the saints . . .."

When the priest or the deacon says: "Commemorating our most holy, pure, blessed and glorified Lady, Theotokos and ever-Virgin Mary, with all the Saints...", our Church directs us to remember its glorious history written in the tears, suffering, and the blood of all the saints.

We have learned what is called "saint," in the previous homily. No one is born a saint; all are born unclean. This great truth was proclaimed in sighs and groans by the God-inspired prophet and psalmist, David, who said: "For behold, I was conceived in iniquities, and in sin did my mother bear me" (Psalm 50:7).

Among the millions and billions of people (who have come and gone from this life), only one was born sinless. He was born not in a natural, but in a supernatural way. He was born of the saint without ancestral sin, without personal sins. He is Holy in an absolute degree. He is the only one who has said: "Which one of you can prove me guilty of sin?" (John 8:46). As our Church chants: "One is Holy, one is Lord, Jesus Christ."

Christ is the Holy One; He is the source of sanctification. He cleanses us from every sin with His precious blood. With his mystery of Baptism and the mystery of

Repentance and Confession, He cleanses us of ancestral sin and from personal sins. With his mystery of Holy Communion, He unites us with Himself, and gives us His divine power.

Christ is our sanctification; Without Him, there is no holiness. The saints are a reflection of His holiness on earth; a great proof (and demonstration) that Christ lives and reigns "to all ages."

Holiness is the main purpose of life, to which the faithful must look and strive to attain, saying: "I want to become a saint, no matter what it will cost me, even if I must suffer martyrdom and shed my blood for the love of Christ!" This desire for holiness existed vividly in the hearts of the early Christians. These Christians hated sin, as men today hate and dislike the terrible illness of cancer, and they loved virtue, as today men desire and love material things.

So the question arises: In our time, is there any appreciation and desire for holiness? Unfortunately today, as the situation now stands, other appreciations and other desires prevail and reign in this world. There are the worldy desires. There is the desire for riches, which causes a young man to leave his beloved village, relatives, and friends, and go abroad, not because he cannot survive in his poor country, but because he wants to become wealthy. "I want to become rich," one says. "I want to become strong and powerful," says another. "I want to be educated and become a scientist," says a third one. Who says today: "I want to become a saint"?

The word 'saint' provokes sarcasm and mockery from the contemporary world. Its ideal is not saintliness. Its ideal is material things, the possession and exploitation of them, the enjoyment of them, the arts and sciences. The latter are not used as a means for the spiritual progress of humanity, but as a means, in most cases, for materialistic prosperity, corruption, and depravity.

Sanctity is despised, mocked, and hated, even by the majority, as though it is something that no longer has a place in this world. Parents want to see their child rich, a scientist, who will enjoy all the material goods of the earth, but not a man of God. If they see that their child shows an inclination towards divine matters, wants to live a true Christian life, and avoid everything which is against the will of God, these parents, instead of being happy, feel upset, worry, and do everything possible to get their child off God's road and onto the devil's. They don't want the child to attend Sunday School, to read Holy Scripture, or to form relationships with pious people.

Though these parents call themselves Christians, they are not. They hate the holiness in the face of their child. They hate God. They might go to church and venerate the icons; but if they see the icon of a saint coming alive in the face of their child, who wants to live the life of the saints, then their real intentions appear. Hypocrites! They venerate the icons of saints, but want to shred into a thousand pieces the icon of holiness which their child is trying to paint with his life. They think: "The saints must remain only in the icons. We must not imitate them and copy them in our lives. No more saints; no more Saints Demetrios, Nicholas, Eustratios, etc.... No more Saints Katherine, Barbara, and Paraskeve. Enough! We do not need any more saints...." These men and women, the way they think, want Christianity to be a dead religion, a religion without any influence in the modern world. "Out of our lives, saints!" This is a sign which means, "Out of our lives Christ!"

Contempt of holiness, aversion and hatred toward the saints. In a certain old church, I saw the eyes dug out of the icons of the saints, which were painted on the walls. I was horrified by this spectacle. Perplexed, I asked how it happened. I knew that during the period of Turkish rule, fanatic Turks used to enter churches and, employing their spears, dig out the eyes of Christ and the All-Holy Virgin. But the eyes of the saints they left untouched. Unfortunately, these eyes were dug out by unbelievers, by atheists who entered the church during the terrible civil war which the nation went through (with the Communists). They desecrated the church and dug out the eyes of the saints. There is no doubt that if these men had lived during the time of the saints, they would not have hesitated to dig out the real eyes of those saints. Hatred for the saints is directed against their holy icons as well.

The unbelievers, the atheists, hate the saints. They do not wish to see them even in icons. By hating the saints, they express their hatred against God. However, despite the disregard, aversion, and hatred which fell towards the saints, old and new, the saints continue to be honored and celebrated. No satanic power will ever succeed in extinguishing pious remembrance of them.

ONE HEAVEN

"Commemorating . . . with all the saints."

We have said in previous homilies that in a period of materialism and corruption, holiness not only is not honored as the highest ideal of life, but is even hated. In continuing our discussion, we are reminded of two other cases, cases which prove the hatred of a world without God towards the saints.

In a village in Macedonia, a girl married a young man who came from a distant place without investigating his beliefs. What horror she experienced when, during the first days of their marriage, the young man grabbed the icons, which were on the home iconostasis, threw them down, and was ready to cast them into the fire! He was a Jehovah's Witness. But the bride believed in Christ. She would not tolerate this. She threw him out. She placed her faith above her husband. And she did well, because she could live without a husband, but not without God.

Another case which shows aversion and hatred towards the saints is a recent decision of an atheistic Balkan state, Albania. There are still tens of thousands of Orthodox Greeks living there, Greeks who inspite of all the persecutions against religion, continue to remain faithful to the religion of their ancestors. All of these believing Orthodox Greeks, men and women alike, have as given names those of saints. This does not please the atheistic regime. It ordered them to change their Christian names to other names foreign to the Christian religion. And as the newspapers are reporting, they have given them a time limit. The trial of our Christian brothers in Albania is great. They are being forced to change their Christian names, names of saints which they have had from generation to generation.

War has been declared against the saints, as the Book of Revelation says so prophetically (12:17; 13:7). War against all that is holy and sacred.

But holiness does not vanish. It is a heavenly tree which sprouts, blooms, and bears fruit in every generation, in every place, in every time. The Church will bear saints till the end of time. Perhaps the saints may be fewer, but they will not vanish. And even in places where we believe that no saints exist, and we are ready to cry out that there are no more saints on earth, the Lord has His people who believe in Him, worship Him, and live according to His will.

Not only those who wear the cassock and live in monasteries can become saints. It is possible for someone to be a monk, a priest, or a bishop and, in spite of this, be in danger of losing his soul and being internally comdemned. As St. Cosmas Aitolos said, only a small number of the clergy will be saved. And it is possible for someone who is a layman, one living in the world, to succeed in overcoming temptations and become a saint, because of his faith and strict Christian way of life. We have saints coming from all classes. We will mention a few examples. St. Tryphon was a farmer, St. Spyridon a shepherd, St. Joseph the Righteous was a carpenter, the Three Hierarchs were teachers, the Forty Martyrs were soldiers, St. Demetrios and St. George were officers, St. Ambrose was a governor, and Sts. Constantine and Helen were monarchs.

Neither the profession, nor the age of the person, nor the epoch and year, hindered the development of the saints. Children and young adults, grownups and white-haired old folks, were sanctified and suffered martyrdom for the glory of Christ, not only in ancient times, but in this century, too. St. Nectarios, for example, the bishop of Pentapolis, is a saint who lived in this century. And only he? There are others, whose names have remained unknown, but are known and written in the Books of God. And no one can erase what is written in God's Books. There are those living in atheistic countries who are persecuted for their Christian faith, are imprisoned, and die the martyr's death. There are also those Christians who, during the disaster in Asia Minor, were beheaded like lambs by the knife of the enemies of the Christian religion, because they refused to abjure their Christian faith and become Moslems.

During the night when we see the sky glittering with stars, we are filled with wonder. But to the faithful, the spectacle of another sky evokes more admiration, that of the spiritual heaven. This spiritual heaven is the Church. Christ is the Sun that never sets. The saints are stars. But, as all stars do not have the same degree of brightness, so the saints differ from one another in the brightness of their sanctity in the spiritual heaven. There are saints who by their exceptional work, wise writings, their struggle in defending the Orthodox faith, their martyrdoms and miracles, glitter like "stars with many lights", stars of the first order. And there are the great fathers and teachers of the Church, to whom the hymnody of the Church refers us: "O brilliant stars of the spiritual heaven."

In addition to these great fathers and teachers of the Church, there are countless other saints who are scattered throughout society, living holy lives in accordance with the Gospel. However, because of the unimportant positions which they hold, they are unheard of in the worldly circles, and pass by unnoticed. "Stars" of this vain world are noticed, such as movie actors and athletes. But who pays attention to the poor Christian head of a family, who lives in this world with faith and fear of God, fathering and raising children in accordance with His will? This hero of life, this contemporary saint, remains obscure. The time will come, however, when these people, small in the eyes of the world, but great in the eyes of God, will shine as the Lord said, like the sun (Matt. 13:43).

Among the unnumerable multitude of the saints, there is one star that shines brighter than all the rest. This star shines like the moon when it is full. It comforts and encourages us. It is the All-Holy Theotokos. For this reason the Church, when it commemorates the saints, first mentions the name of the All-Holy Virgin. "Commemorating our most holy, pure, most blessed, glorified Lady Theotokos and Ever-Virgin Mary..."

With God's help, we will speak about the most holy Theotokos in another place in the Divine Liturgy. And so now, finishing our homilies on the saints, we say that all the saints who are in heaven with Christ show a deep interest in the Christians who are here on earth, and from on high they pray for us who are striving in the difficult struggle for faith and virtue. Our Orthodox faith teaches us that the prayers of the saints, the faithful servants of the Lord, are being heard by God, and miracles do take place here on earth. Truly, "Wondrous is God in His saints" (Psalm 67:36).

By the intercessions of the Theotokos and of all of the saints, O Saviour, save us.

OUR SECURITY

"Let us commend ourselves and one another and our whole life to Christ our God."

The first created man and woman, as long as they obeyed the Heavenly Father, lived peacefully in paradise and had a sense of security. But when they disobeyed God's commandment, they lost the feeling of security, along with everything else. In the same way a misbehaving child is afraid when he hears his father coming, so Adam and Eve trembled when they heard God's voice, and ran to hide.

Since then, sinful man has lived in anxiety, agitation and insecurity, because he has separated himself from his Heavenly Father. And man, because of his anxiety, tries to find his own way and build his own sheltering castles, in order to feel secure.

When the great flood came, no summit or mountain was safe. Security existed only in Noah's Ark. But after many years had passed men multiplied again. Men began to sin, became anxious and troubled, and thought that they could protect themselves from a new danger of destruction. They decided to build a tower so tall that its top would reach the sky, and inside it they could find security. But as Scripture says, while building the tower, the confusion of the languages took place, and they did not succeed in finishing it (Gen. 11:1-9).

As those men were trying to find security in their tower, so all people living a worldly life, using various ways and means, try to secure themselves in their own towers. Remember the foolish rich man of the Lord's parable (Luke 12:16-21). His fields yielded an exceptional harvest. The harvest was so great, that the crops would not fit in his barns. He became anxious. He was afraid that if the rich harvest remained outside it would be lost. That's why he had to find a way to protect his crops, so that no thief could touch them. And so he decided to tear down his store houses and build larger ones. Then he could live happily for many years on the goods which he had safely stored. His security, therefore, was assured by his warehouses. But he was unable to bring his plan into being, for the great thief appeared. And this great thief who enters homes and takes the most expensive and precious thing, life, is called death. He came that night and took the foolish rich man of the parable. This makes it clear that his riches did not secure the happiness of his life.

But even today, how many people do not regard wealth as the security of their life? They work hard, they sweat, they try by every means, even the most unfair, to make money. And when they make it, they put it in various banks, businesses and trusts, thinking that with this money they will secure the future for themselves and their children. But how mistaken they are! For as experience testifies, when wars, troubles, and revolutions take place, even the rich banks close. The currency, loosing its value, fails, and causes factories and buildings to change owners in a day. Where is their security? The tower that they build gets torn down.

But behold! Others are building, in our own age, another tower which shines and rises, reaching to the stars. This tower, which dazzles the eyes of humanity with its grandeur, is science. People are seeking their security in this tower. But even this one is not firm. Science can build a big city, equip it with all the conveniences: streets, squares, water-systems, bright lighting. But one night a powerful earthquake brings it all down and buries thousands of people in its ruins. Where is security?

There are others, trying to obtain security for themselves by means of various political systems which promise a happy future to humanity. They are building their own towers, too. But these politico-economic towers do not take long to get torn down, leaving the people greatly disturbed and in anguish. Would you like to see one of these kinds of towers? It is the alliances. It is the organizations of the United Nations. It is the Security Councils. The suffering people (of this world) think that in them they will find security. But only one example – that of tragic Cyprus – testifies that in these big organizations there is no security.

The security of our life and of our future as individuals, families, nations, and mankind, does not exist in money, or science, or in alliances with big and powerful states and international organizations. Security exists somewhere else. It is found where men do not seek it. And even if they hear about this kind of security, they mock and laugh at it, just as people mocked and laughed at Noah, when they saw him building his ark of security against the cataclysm. But these mockeries and ironies should not stop us from crying out loud that the safety and security of us all is *God*.

Yes, God. The Church commands us to entrust all our lives and whatever is valuable and precious to the omnipotent God. This is the meaning of the admonition: "Let us commend ourselves and one another and our whole life to Christ our God," as well as the exclamation which follows: "For to Thee belongs all glory, honor and worship, to the Father, and to the Son, and to the Holy Spirit, now and forever and from all ages to all ages."

My dear friends! People run to secure their valuables in bank vaults. Let those of us who believe, imitate the example to true Christians and entrust our precious treasures, our immortal souls, to Christ. To thee, O Lord! Yes, to Thee, O Christ, we entrust everything. You are our life, our salvation, and our security.

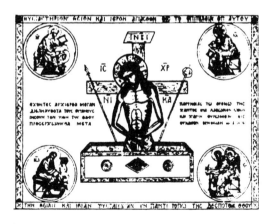

DEDICATION

"To Thee, O Lord".

The Church, at the end of the great supplication, addresses itself to all the communicants and exhorts them, having in mind the example of the Saints and particularly the All-Holy Mother of God, to imitate their virtues and entrust their life and the lives of others to Christ. "Let us commend ourselves and one another and our whole life to Christ our God."

To this command of the Church, the pious people reply with the words, "To Thee, O Lord." This answer is our pledge to Christ; we trust Him and we dedicate our existence to Him.

Confidence and dedication in Christ. But I wonder if we carry out whatever we pledge to Christ during the Divine Liturgy. We have seen in the previous homily what it means to have confidence in Christ. Now, in this homily, we will see what it means to dedicate ourselves to Christ.

Dedication means that we promise to God something which belongs to us, and from that moment on, we cannot take it back. For example, a holy chalice is given by a donor to the church to be used by the priest for the offering of the Holy Eucharist. This chalice, being a gift to the church, cannot be taken back home by its owner and used as a common cup, something to give him amusement or pleasure while drinking. Such an act is called desecration and is considered to be one of the greatest acts of impiety. Divine and human laws punish impious men. This desecration was committed by an ancient king of the Babylonians, Belteshazzar. His father, Nebuchadnezzar, when he conquered Jerusalem, took the sacred vessels for the Temple of Solomon. They were fashioned with great skill from gold and silver and were very expensive. Nebuchadnezzar kept them as precious treasures. But his son, Belteshazzar, during a festival which he held at the palace, ordered the sacred vessels to be brought out and used as cups for a treat for the guests. The sacred vessels became wine cups. God's punishment for this desecration came immediately (Daniel 5).

People in the Old Testament dedicated gold and silver items to God, as today there are Christians who dedicate censers, chalices, etc. to the churches. But these are not the great and important dedications for which the new religion, Christianity, asks. The Christian spirit is asking for something more valuable than these material gifts. More than gold, silver and precious stones. And this is not outside ourselves. It is our own self. It is our souls, our body, our heart, our thoughts, our feelings, our will. It is our entire existence.

God is asking us to dedicate our whole being to Him. And as it is forbidden to use a holy chalice for any other purpose besides the Divine Liturgy, in the same way, it is forbidden for us to use our body and our entire existence for sinful purposes. Only for God's – namely, to do His holy will during our whole life. This is what the first commandment tells us. "You must love the Lord your God with all your heart, and with all your soul, and

with all your mind" (Deut. 6:4-5; Matt. 22:37). For someone to dedicate himself to God is the greatest thing which
a person can do. Other things, which are outside of
himself, like houses, farms, diamonds and other precious
stones, are not difficult to promise and to dedicate. But
for someone to dedicate his entire being to God and to
follow all of the commandments is so difficult, and such
a great undertaking, that only a few succeed in doing
this in their lifetime.

However, this is the kind of dedication which Christ
asks from all of us, as an indispensible condition, in order
to be counted under His glorious flag.

The Church asks this kind of dedication from each
one of us. Before a person is baptized, the priest performing the sacrament asks two very important questions.
The first is this: "Do you renounce satan and all his angels
and all his pomp?" The baptismal candidate, or his godfather if he is an infant, responds saying three times, "I
do renounce him," namely, I do not want to have any
relationship with the devil. I hate him and I turn my face
against him, and whatever belongs to him. I discontinue
doing his will. Definitely, I break relationships with him.
The second question the priest asks the candidate for
Baptism is: "Do you join Christ?" And the candidate or
godfather responds: "I do join Him," namely, I belong
now to Christ, and I will try to do His holy will
throughout my whole life.

This is the sacred promise which we give to Christ
in the Church before the sacrament of Baptism begins.
We must remember this sacred promise always and
never allow our body and soul to become soiled – let's
say – with sin, by doing the will of satan.

However, what a pity! We forget this sacred promise;
evil carries us away, we fall into various sins and infect
ourselves. By that which we say in the Divine Liturgy,
"To Thee, O Lord," we renew this sacred promise of Baptism and say before the angels and archangels:

"O Christ! We put all our trust in Thee. To Thee we
give all our love and dedication. To Thee I dedicate all
my existence and even my life itself. I am ready for all
sacrifice for Thy love – I am Thine. To Thee, O Lord."

"O my Christ! Illuminate us, so that when we hear,
'To Thee, O Lord,' our hearts will be inflamed with divine
love and our dedication will be a real, lifelong and eternal 'To Thee, O Lord.' "

ALL GLORY

"For to Thee belong all glory, honor and worship to the Father, and to the Son, and to the Holy Spirit, now and forever and from all ages to all ages."

In our previous homily, we explained the "To Thee, O Lord." These words, as we have said, are of the greatest importance. Our whole life belongs to Christ. To Him we give all our trust and devotion.

After the "To Thee, O Lord," which the chanter says on behalf of the congregation, the priest is heard to say in a loud voice: "For to Thee belong all glory, honor and worship, to the Father, and to the Son, and to the Holy Spirit, now and forever and from all ages to all ages."

We can consider this exclamation as either the conclusion of the great supplication, or as a sentence which explains the content of a beautiful prayer that the priest reads. A third explanation is that it is neither connected with the great supplication nor with the prayer which the priest reads, but is, as Fr. Gervasios Paraskevopoulos (that excellent interpreter of the Divine Liturgy) said, a kind of doxology to the Triune God.

"Glory to the Father, and to the Son, and to the Holy Spirit." This is heard not once, but many times during the Divine Liturgy. Because, as we said when explaining the beginning of the Divine liturgy, the "Blessed be the Kingdom of the Father, and of the Son, and of the Holy

Spirit....," the doctrine of the Holy Trinity is very important; it is the most precious dogma of our faith.

Father, Son, and Holy Spirit is the Truine God of the Christians. One God, but three persons. This is a great and incomprehensible mystery. This mystery was unknown to the men of the Old Testament. There are only a few quotations concerning the Holy Trinity, which like a bright sun, starts to send its rays to illuminate the hearts of man. But whatever was veiled and dark to the ancient world and even to the Hebrews themselves, became clear and shining when Christ came into the world. God manifested Himself at the Jordan River, when Christ was baptized. For this reason, the day of Christ's Baptism in the Jordan was named Theophania, God's manifestation. As our Church sings so beautifully: "At Your Baptism in the Jordan River, O Lord, the worship due to the Holy Trinity was made manifest . . .."

Many unbelievers do not accept the doctrine of the Holy Trinity. They say that they cannot understand how the One is Three and the Three are One. St. Augustine, one of the greatest minds of humankind, gives an answer to these unbelievers of both ancient and modern times. This saint wished to investigate this great mystery. But his mind became confused from deep thinking while he pondered these things. So he came out of his study to take a walk by the seashore. There, he saw a charming boy playing. The child dug a hole in the sandy beach, then took his little bucket to get water from the sea and poured it into the hole.

"What are you doing there, my boy?" the saint asked.

And the small child answered: "Do you see the sea? I will empty it by pouring all its water into this hole!"

"But this, my boy, is impossible," the saint said.

"Oh", answered the child, "if it is impossible for me to empty the sea with my little bucket, it is incomparably more difficult for you, with your small mind, to understand the mystery of the Holy Trinity."

The child who spoke thus was an angel. We have told you this anecdote before, but it is so instructive that it is worth hearing again (see p. 34).

"Glory to the Father and to the Son and to the Holy Spirit." The teaching about the Holy Trinity used to move the Christians. Upon hearing the name of the Holy Trinity, their hearts used to beat faster, their eyes shed tears, and to their lips would come very sweet words, with which they tried to demonstrate their boundless reverence and love for the Holy Trinity, Who saved the world. Yes, the Father through the Son and the Holy Spirit created the world, reformed and saved man. The persons of the Holy Trinity are united. When one person is mentioned, the Father or the Son or the Holy Spirit, immediately the other two persons are thought of.

"Glory to the Father, and to the Son and to the Holy Spirit." All the Fathers of the Church speak of the Holy Trinity. But the father who spoke the most about the Holy Trinity, correctly interpreting the passages of Holy Scripture, both the Old and New Testament, who supported the teachings about the Holy Trinity and defeated the heretics that fought against it, was St. Gregory of Nazianzos, who because of this was named "Theologian." O Holy Trinity save Thy world and me! This is how he ends one of his homilies.

To the Holy Trinity belongs "all glory." The Holy Trinity must be praised and glorified not only now, but also "forever and from all ages to all ages."

The teaching about the Holy Trinity shines like a spiritual sun from the beginning to the end of the Divine Liturgy. In the bright light of the Holy Scriptures the Divine Liturgy is celebrated. This is the reason that the doxology to the Holy Trinity is heard so often during the Liturgy.

All glory to the Holy Trinity. But the question arises: Is the Holy Trinity actually praised and glorified in our country? Are we touched? What happens to us when we hear the name of the Holy Trinity?

The Holy Trinity is honored in the Greek Constitution, the most official document of our State. It starts with the Holy Trinity: "In the name of the Holy and consubstantial and undivided Trinity." All of our constitutions since the time of our liberation have started this way. And the Greeks, by writing the name of the Holy Trinity at the frontispiece of our Constitution, want to show to the whole world that above all we have faith in the Holy Trinity, and that nothing exists which is more precious to us in this world.

But unfortunately, while the Holy Trinity is honored at the beginning of the Constitution, in other expressions of individual, familial, communal and ethnic concerns, it is not honored.

Oh! Holy Trinity have mercy on us and on the whole world. Glory to Thee!

II

THE ANTIPHONS

PSALMODY

After the exclamation by the priest: "For to Thee belong all glory, honor and worship to the Father...," the first antiphon is sung. The second antiphon is sung after the exclamation of the priest: "For Thine is the dominion and Thine is the Kingdom and the power and the glory of the Father...." The third antiphon is sung after the priest exclaims: "For Thou art a good and man-loving God, and to Thee we ascribe glory, to the Father...."

The first antiphon is: "Bless the Lord, O my soul...;" and the second is: "Praise the Lord, O my soul...;" and the third consists of the Beatitudes of the Lord. At the end of the first antiphon is sung the refrain: "By the intercessions of the Theotokos, O Saviour, save us,". At the end of the second antiphon, the second refrain: " O Son of God, Who didst rise from the dead, save us who chant to Thee: Alleluia," is chanted, – and also the hymn: "O only-begotten Son...." And at the end of the third antiphon the Apolytikion of the Sunday is sung.

Today the antiphons are often omitted. Usually, only the refrains are chanted: "By the intercessions of the Mother of God...," and: "O Son of God Who didst rise from the dead...," as well as the Apolytikion of the Sunday.

But before we examine the antiphons, let us see what the word "antiphon" means.

The Christian who goes to church today hears three or four voices. The first is the deacon, the second is the priest, the third is the bishop and the fourth is the cantor, alternating. No other voices are heard.

But what is happening today did not happen in the ancient church of the first centuries in the catacombs. There the voice of the people was heard. One voice, which came from the heart of the people. One voice, which at times sounded like thunder. This thunder was the voice of the people attending church. Men, women and small children participated in some of the parts of the psalmody and accompanied the chanters in the singing of the most important hymns. St. John Chrysostom says that the first one who introduced the common chanting of psalms into the Church was St. Ignatius, bishop of Antioch, who for his confession of faith was thrown into the arena of Rome and was eaten by the hungry lions. This saint saw a vision. He saw angels, formed into two opposing choirs, antiphonically singing very sweet songs glorifying the Holy Trinity, by taking turns one after the other. From this vision, St. Ignatius was inspired to separate the congregation into two parts. Also, St Ephraim the Syrian, one of the sweetest melodists of the Church, introduced the antiphonic system into the churches. And also St. Basil the Great, as noted in a letter of his, introduced the antiphonic system into his diocese. The congregation used to be divided into two parts and accompanied the designated chanters in the psalmody. The chanters would start the psalmody and would give the signal for the others to sing along.

St. John Chrysostom also speaks on this subject, saying clearly that when the designated chanters sing the antiphons, the people who are in the church, the men, women, and children, are to unite their voices with the voices of the chanters. Thus, the people participated in the Divine Liturgy. The People were not simple spectators, but in a particular way played their role in the great drama called the Divine Liturgy. What grandeur! What mystery! Inside the Divine Liturgy all voices of the angels, archangels, archpriests, priests, deacons, men, women and children were united. One divine harp with many chords, each chord having its own grace. Hearing such a Divine Liturgy, one had the feeling that he was not touching the earth, but was in heaven. Even unbelievers, upon entering such a church, were touched, believed, and repented.

Psalms and hymns were chanted antiphonically in the ancient church. This way of chanting awoke even the most nonchalant. The same thing was used by the military in guardhouses; soldiers, in order to maintain their vigilance, called back and forth to each other: "Guardians, be vigilant." By calling back and forth to each other, they were speaking antiphonically. In the same way, the Christians attending church, by chanting psalms and hymns antiphonically, were kept in spiritual wakefulness.

The ancient church sang antiphonically. But this antiphonic system has been discontinued in the contemporary church. It is preserved in a few monasteries, where pious monks keep vigils during the night and sing antiphonically. But in the churches of the cities and villages, only the voice of the chanters is heard. The voice of the people is not heard, and we can see the results.

The chanters psalmodize, but who from the congregation is paying attention to what is being sung? Not the congregants. Their minds are wandering here and there. They appear cold and indifferent. Many start discussions with those next to them. The ones who hear the Divine Liturgy are the chanters and the priests. And even they only listen with their ears. They stand before the awesome mystery with coldness and indifference, even as so many dramatic scenes develop before them. They are like, as we have said before, records playing on a gramaphone. As the Divine Liturgy is celebrated now, the mystery of the Liturgy certainly takes place, but the souls are not touched and these souls leave the church spiritually unsatisfied.

This situation must not continue. A holy revolution should take place in the Liturgical area. This holy revolution should not add or subtract parts of the Divine Liturgy, as some modernists propose, but should return to the ancient custom of the early Church. The pious faithful must not continue to appear like silent and dumb persons in the church, but must participate in some way in the Divine Liturgy, chanting certain psalms and hymns glorifying the Holy Trinity, as well as the "amen," the "Kyrie eleison," the "To Thee, O Lord," the cherubic hymn, reciting the "Creed," the "Our Father," etc. And because illiterate people are not in a position to chant, pious teachers must teach the children of the elementary school to chant at certain times in the Divine Liturgy, chanting these parts which we have just mentioned. Thus, the antiphonic system can be reinstated. For when the children get used to the system, and they grow up, it will not be difficult to chant antiphonically again.

God grant that we who are pained by the appearance of contemporary holy worship, should work for the return of that ancient practice. The antiphon is one of the evidences of the magnificence of Orthodox worship.

PROPHECIES

We have spoken previously, beloved, about both the moral and religious situation before the coming of Christ. People had forgotten the true God, and had fallen into idol worship. Their gods became the sun, the moon, the stars, the rivers and the seas. They had fallen into such an abyss of error that they worshipped cats, dogs, frogs and snakes. Even the animals had become their gods. There was nothing which they did worship as god. This may seem unbelievable to you, but the idols which the archaeologists have discovered speak for themselves. Idolatry, in its worst forms, predominated in the world.

Do not think that only the barbarous and uncivilized peoples who lived in caves and tilled the ground with their nails and pointed stones were the only true idol worshippers. Even those who had built magnificant buildings and great civilizations, such as the Greeks and Romans, fell down and worshipped idols. Athens and Rome, the most famous and largest of the ancient cities, were full of them. This current of idolatry was so powerful that even those people who knew the true God, the Hebrews, often became so carried away that they left the worship of Him, and bowed before idols, as is mentioned in the history of the Prophet Elias (3 Kings, chapters 18-19) and elsewhere in the Old Testament.

Insofar as the question of religion is concerned, this period was the midnight of mankind. As at nighttime, when the sun disappears and the darkness has spread itself everywhere, the stars throw a little light, the darkness lessens, and man has hope and is consoled that the light has not been lost forever. And so it was during the dark night of idolatry; some stars were visible. Wise men appeared in the depths of the spiritual darkness of the ancient world, and having been illuminated by the true God, like the stars, shed a bit of light by word and example. And so men's souls were consoled, and they could hope that the spiritual light had not completely disappeared. These inspired men were mainly prophets, such as David and Elias, and the four great and the twelve lesser prophets.

The prophecies of these inspired men made a great impression. Despairing men listened with joy, when they heard that a new period of happiness would come to the world. Every prophecy was like a bright star. But as the stars differ from each other in brightness, so also some prophecies differed from the others; some shone like stars of the first order. When reading the prophecies of the Old Testament, you can easily see that some are clear predictions of various events in the Gospel, such as the birth of Christ from a virgin, His baptism in the Jordan River, His preaching and miracles, and certain prominent details of His crucifixion and resurrection.

At this point, someone is probably wondering why we are speaking about ancient idolatry and prophets while explaining the Divine Liturgy. What have they to do with this? They have, beloved, a definite relationship, and I ask you to pay close attention.

The divine Liturgy presents the whole mystery of Divine providence. It presents our Lord Jesus Christ. He is the spiritual light of mankind. Just as before the dawn-

ing of sun when the earth was enveloped in darkness,
with only the stars casting a little light, in the same way
before Christ's coming, a spiritual darkness reigned and
only the prophets shed a little light on the world. Because
the Divine Liturgy is a representation of the life of Christ,
and mainly of His sacrifice on the Cross, before the
presentation of Christ's Passion and sacrifice it presents
Christ as the Teacher. But even before it presents Christ
the Teacher preaching us the Gospel, it presents the prophets, who foretold His coming to the world, His life
and His Passion.

Let us clarify this in a better way. The Divine Liturgy
ends with Christ's triumph and His Ascension. But before
the Ascension there is the Resurrection. Before the
Resurrection there is the Cross. Before the Cross there
is the Mystical Supper. Before the Mystical Supper there
is the preaching of Christ and of the apostles. Before the
Gospel and the Apostolos, namely before we hear Christ
and the apostles preach the Gospel of salvation, the
Divine Liturgy invites us to hear the voice of the prophets who foretold the sunrise from the depths of
mankind's darkness. The Christian who attends the
Divine Liturgy sees with the eyes of his soul a wonderous
film unfolding before him, filled with scenes from
Christ's life, and he hears the voices of angels, prophets
and apostles speaking about Him.

After the great supplication, which we have already
explained, are the antiphons. In the ancient Church these
were the prophetic readings, taken from the books of
the prophets. While the Christians were hearing these
readings, they were preparing themselves to hear the
readings from the Apostolos and the Gospel. This shows
that the writers of the Divine Liturgy were not common

men. They were men of God, inspired men who put everything in the Divine Liturgy in its proper place. The Liturgy resembles a wondrous edifice of stone, each piece fitting perfectly.

In the ancient Church, the antiphons were not always the same prophecies. The priest had the right to select whichever psalm he considered best for the spiritual needs of the people. Later, three antiphons were used, and were designated beforehand. This first antiphon became Psalm 102 (103 in King James Version) — "Blessed the Lord, O my soul;" the second became Psalm 145 (146) — "Praise the Lord, O my soul...;" and the third antiphon became the Beatitudes of the Lord.

We will discuss these antiphons later. For the present, since we are at the end of this homily, let us thank the Lord, Who enables us to hear the Divine Liturgy every Sunday.

"BLESS THE LORD, O MY SOUL"

The first antiphon, as we said in the previous homily, beloved, is a hymn from the Book of Psalms, which is a collection made by David. It is a holy bouquet, consisting of immortal flowers; one hundred and fifty psalms spreading their spiritual fragrance. Many of them are prophetic, because they speak about Christ, the Messiah of the world, and praise His grandeur.

In past times, the Book of Psalms was one of the most loved books of our people. These Christians knew the Psalter from childhood, many by heart, and quoted sayings from it throughout all the various situation of their lives. We highly recommend to you the Psalter which contains the short interpretations of the learned Professor Panayotes Trempelas. Keep it under your pillow, and read it before going to sleep.

The first antiphon is the 102nd Psalm (103rd in King James English version). This psalm begins with the verse: "Bless the Lord, O my soul, and all that is within me bless His Holy name."

Among all other evils and vices which man has is that of ingratitude. This is especially true in the twentieth century. He is ungrateful to his parents, to his teachers, to his benefactors, and most importantly, he is ungrateful to his greatest benefactor, God. As the fish lives in water and cannot survive outside of it, so man lives in the sea of God's benefactions, and without them he is unable to survive. He should be grateful to God and express this gratitude to his Benefactor.

Man, however, forgets God's benevolence. Hours, days, months, years, and even an entire lifetime pass, and the ungrateful do not say even one "thank you" to God. Not only does he not say "thank you," but, alas, he opens his mouth and blasphemes his Creator. "Instead of manna, gall; instead of water, vinegar."

The 102nd Psalm reminds people of God's benefactions. The psalmist places a list before the ungrateful, full of God's most important benevolences. He shows his catalog to all, starting with himself. It is as if he says: O people! Read this list and see how many benefactions God has performed in your life. And when you remember these countless benevolences, your heart will be moved and you will open your mouth and bless God: "Bless the Lord, O my soul, and all that is within me, bless His holy name."

"Bless the Lord, O my soul." Do you want to see God's benefactions in more detail? Look "within" you, as the psalmist says. What is "within?" A human being is visible and invisible; a visible body and an invisible soul. If we consider the "within" in relationship to the body, then the "within" of man's organism includes the heart, lungs, kidneys, veins, arteries, nerves, five sensory organs, etc. Examine each part carefully, and you will marvel at their Creator. With how much wisdom did He create them! The heart, for example is an excellent pump, works by itself, and does this unceasingly, so long as a man lives. The kidneys are excellent filters, the eyes are a superb camera. The ears are like radar. Signs of gratitude are sent to God from all parts of the bodily existence. A man must thank God for their good functioning.

Not only is there the "within the body," but there is also the "within the soul." There are the spiritual and psychological functions: the mind, memory, imagination, feeling, will. All these must move towards God in praise and glorification.

"Bless the Lord, O my soul, and all that is within me bless His holy name." There is also another matter for which we must be thankful to God. People have a variety of desires and needs. What are the desires and needs of the body? Let us list some of them. Is man thirsty? To satisfy this need God created fountains of water, rivers, lakes; and man quenches his thirst with the clear waters. Is man hungry? God created trees and plants, and man gets his food from them, satisfying his hunger. Is man naked and suffering from the cold? God took care of even this need; man makes clothes and coverings from raw materials, such as cotton and wool. Is man sick, thereby in danger? God took care that certain plants of the earth have properties, which, with the help of science, become medicine. Our good God takes care of all man's desires and needs. This is the reason why the psalmist thanks God "Who fulfilleth thy desire with good things."

There are other kinds of needs besides the desires and needs of the body. There are the desires and needs of the soul. What are these? Let us see. The soul sins. Then it feels guilty, which is the pressure of sin. It groans, and begs for mercy and forgiveness. It asks forgiveness of God; and God, who could punish man immediately for his sins, shows His endless love towards man, the creation of His own hands. He pities him, He shows compassion and grants forgiveness. As the psalmist says, "Compassionate and merciful is the Lord, longsuffering and plenteous in mercy; not unto the end will He be angered, neither unto eternity will He be wroth. Not according to our iniquities has He dealt with us, neither according to our sins hath He rewarded us." I ask you: Is there any greater benefaction than forgiveness of man's sins by God? Tell me who, no matter how sinful he is, upon hearing this psalm, is not consoled with the thought that God, like a loving father, is ready to forgive all his sins?

"Bless the Lord, O my soul." When a person remembers God's benevolent acts towards his soul and body, his gratitude overflows and he cries out not only to other people, but to the angels, and to the entire celestial and earthly creation to join him in hymning the boundless love of God.

GOD'S STATE

When, beloved, a people get organized and acquire a government, an army and navy, then we say that this people has become a state. It acquired power and strength and can back-up (and support) its citizens. Its citizens, wherever they find themselves in the world, can take refuge in their embassy and ask their country's help. How much emotion a foreigner feels, when in a large city he sees the flag of his country waving at its embassy! "My country will support my rights," says the immigrant who has been wronged in a foreign land.

There are many states. The citizens of each state boast about their country. Some of them because their state possesses vast lands, great plains, and rivers. Some because their state has a powerful fleet, both mercantile and military, and its flag dominates the high seas. Some because their state promotes science and has the finest universities. Others because their state has developed industry. There are also states whose citizens boast of the glorious history of their ancestors, and of their monuments.

Many states. Which one of them is the most powerful? In our time since the Second World War, two states became very powerful, they acquired such tremendous power that they are called: "superpowers." They are the United States and Russia. The citizens of these states have something of the haughty and egotistic about them;

they see others as inferiors and themselves as the lords of the world. Who dares to touch a citizen of Russia and America? The government of his nation is ready to protest and send ultimatums. Even war is threatened for insults and injustices against their citizens. Citizens of small nations, in order to have strong backing, change citizenship, and how great is their joy when in their hands they have identification proving that they are citizens of America. "An American," says the fellow, who is now under the protective umbrella of that superpower.

But beyond these states, there is another one, incomparably superior to any or all which have appeared or will appear on earth. This is God's state. Who can measure its boundaries, describe its power and its wealth? It surpasses that of even our fantasy. It is dizzying when a person sits down and considers the power and the glory of God's state.

Let us give an example. On this planet, the earth, there are more than one hundred and fifty small and large states. Up until now, not one of them has been able to subjugate all the others, and dominate the entire earth. But if we were to assume that one state did subjugate everyone, this still would not be such a great and important thing, because it suffices for someone only to think that besides this earth there are millions and billions of other planets, bigger than earth, spread throughout the endless universe. Do you know what the earth is if we compare it with them? It is like a small ball with which children play in the school-yard. The astronauts who flew to the moon saw the earth appearing like a ball. And if they could fly still further, the earth would disappear from their eyes, not to be seen at all. Who can tell where the United States, Russia, or the other countries are from up there? When a proud young man boasted about his father's riches to Socrates, in order to teach the boy a lesson, Socrates showed him a map and asked him to point out Athens. This the youth did easily. But when Socrates asked him where the houses and farms of his father were located, the youth could not tell him, for they were not marked on the map.

Borders of states are limited. They are measured out by the square mile and are recorded in atlases. But the borders of God's state are unlimited. God dominates not only one globe, the earth, but all the millions of globes which are moving in infinity.

Blessed, therefore, is the man who becomes naturalized in God's state, in the Kingdom of the Father, of the Son, and of the Holy Spirit. He is under the protection of the omnipotent, all-wise and all-kind God. God- He is the rich one, far surpassing every rich man.

"What? God is rich?" some might say. "Are you not giving attributes to God which more properly belong to the language of the 'bourgeois,' people who are living in riches and care nothing about the poor? You have created God according to your capitalistic ideas. As for us, we will fight this God of the 'bourgeois' and will topple Him, because He is presented as the friend and protector of the rich...!" This some say and write in books, who want to present themselves as intelligent.

How they misrepresent things! God, whom Christ revealed, the true God, is rich. Yes! But rich in the deepest and most noble way; rich, that is to say, in love, for which there is no measure big enough for anyone to measure it with. And it is not only simply a misunderstanding and misconception, but a blasphemy to conceive of God as an image of a rich man, living in greed and avarice, and wronging the poor.

God is "rich in mercy" (Ephes. 2:4), rich in unmeasurable love; rich is He, who spreads all His blessings upon this ungrateful earth. If we people wanted to imitate His love, and all of us obeyed Him, God's state would prevail over all the earth, a state which could solve all the problems of life and would be an image of paradise. But unfortunately, we do not want to belong to God's state; we want to belong to the state of the devil, who governs almost all of humanity by sin and error, and for this reason is called "ruler of the world."

Let us all, therefore, be naturalized in the state of God, and in hymns praise its grandeur.

These meanings, beloved, are included in that beautiful prayer which the celebrant priest says at the end of the great supplication. Let us hear it:

"O Lord our God, Whose might is invincible, Whose glory in incomprehensible, Whose mercy is immeasurable, and Whose love towards mankind is unspeakable; do Thou, O Master, according to Thy goodness, look down upon us and upon this Holy House, and show to us and to those who pray with us Thine abundant mercy and compassion."

SMALL SUPPLICATION

"Again and again in peace let us pray to the Lord."

After the priest says aloud: "For to Thee belong all glory, honor and worship, to the Father, and to the Son, and to the Holy Spirit, now and forever and from all ages to all ages," the "Amen," and the first antiphon: "By the intercessions of the Mother of God...," the small supplication is said: "Again and again in peace let us pray to the Lord," "Help us, save us, have mercy on us and protect us, O God, by Thy Grace," "Commemorating our most Holy, pure, most blessed...."

Now we will discuss this small supplication.

First of all it is called the small supplication to distinguish it from the other, which is called the great. The great supplication as we have seen in our previous homilies contains many petitions. In them we have asked the Triune God not to forsake us, but in His mercy to be always with us, and to give us whatever is necessary and useful for our physical and spiritual life. For man cannot live either spiritually or physically without God's mercy and His love. As we have explained: "For in Him we live and move and have our being" (Acts 17:28).

While the great supplication is a long prayer, the small supplication is a short one, a summary of the great: it is an exhortation for intense prayer. Not just once, but over and over we must pray to God for His mercy. "Again and again."

Beloved, we are living in an age where most people disregard prayer. They think that prayer is useless and obsolete in this contemporary, busy, and noisy world. They say that it is an occupation for those who have nothing else to do. Let the monks, elderly, the sick and the children pray. The rest of us are busy from morning to evening; we don't have the time for such things, they say.

But those who say this and try to take prayer away from modern man miss the point. They are not thinking correctly. Men of our times who are educated, active people who are successful in the arts, sciences, and public life – not the lazy, jobless, illiterate men of past times – confess that prayer is not obsolete and useless as the atheists maintain, but is necessary and useful. One of these men, a scientist and doctor known throughout the world, Carrel, wrote a small book entitled *Prayer*. This famous writer calls prayer a necessity of life, as based on his many observations.

People need to be continuously in communication with the supernatural world, heaven. Man needs God. Carrel characterizes all those who don't pray as cripples. The crippled are those who have lost their vision and cannot see the beauties of the earth. The crippled are those who have lost their hearing and cannot hear the tones of the sweet music. A cripple is someone who has lost one of the five senses. Are these people unfortunate? Not as unfortunate as the one who is not praying; the one who never lifts up his eyes towards heaven, who has lost the most important of all his senses, the sense of faith, and who is living and wallowing in darkness.

Prayer is a most basic need of the soul. Unfortunately, modern man is possessed by matter and is preoccupied with his enjoyment of materialistic things and pleasures, and has destroyed his sacred sense. He is like someone who has a broken antenna on his television set; this person cannot see what the others with working sets can see. Prayer is an antenna which connects us with heaven; now we can see the grandeur of God, adore Him and thank Him.

Yes, prayer is the way we enter into a relationship with God; from it we get invincible power, a supernatural one, and are consoled, illuminated, and strengthened to overcome all the obstacles of life. Yes, prayer is a spiritual weapon: it is an omnipotent weapon of the soul. Yes, prayer. But which prayer? Certainly not just any kind of prayer, but prayer in the way which Christ taught. One of the characteristics of true prayer is perseverance and persistence.

What do we mean by saying perseverance and persistence? There are some Christians who pray and think that whatever they are asking for will immediately be fulfilled. They don't persist in their prayer. As a certain author states, they are like the small children who go knock at a door of a neighboring home and leave immediately. But, the person who really wants to see someone does not knock on the door only once; he knocks many times. In the same way, the Christian who asks God for something which is in agreement with His holy will must not be discouraged when he does not immediately receive what he asked for in his petition. He must be persistent. He must ring the bell continuously, asking for God's mercy.

God, being an affectionate father, listens. But if He delays giving us the thing which we are asking for, He does so not from indifference but because He has His secret purpose. The heavenly Father knows when and how He will give it to us. But we must knock continuously at the door of His mercy. We must pray not just once, but many times, with faith, with persistence and with perseverance. Our Lord taught us this. Open the Holy Scripture and read the first lines of the 18th chapter of the Gospel according to St. Luke. And so the Church teaches us also with the small supplication, admonishing: "Again and again in peace let us pray to the Lord."

"PRAISE THE LORD, O MY SOUL"

The Divine Liturgy is so rich in intent, and includes so many deep and profound meanings, that no matter how many homilies one were to write, it would be impossible to exaust it. It is like a deep well, full of refreshing and cool water, water which never dries up. Unfortunately, people, because of their ignorance and indifference, do not appreciate this spiritual fountain.

After the small petition "Again and again in peace...," which we interpreted in our previous homily, the priest says aloud: "For Thine is the dominion and Thine is the Kingdom and the Power and the Glory of the Father and of the Son and of the Holy Spirit, now and forever and from all ages." This pronouncement is a short glorification of the Triune God.

After this, according to the ancient order of the Church, the second antiphon is sung. This is the 145th Psalm. Its first verses are: "Praise the Lord, O my soul. I will praise the Lord in my life, I will chant unto my God for as long as I have my being." We devote this homily to this psalm.

Prayer is difficult for a person who is not accustomed to it and has not felt its sweetness. Few are those souls who feel the sweetness of prayer and spend hours and hours praying. And the other people? Oh, the others! We must first capture ourselves, then force ourselves to pray. We have to expel the demon of indolence who always finds thousands of excuses for us to use as an escape from the sacred duty of prayer. The command of Christ must be heard in the ears of our souls. "Keep watch and pray, so you will not fall into temptation" (Matt. 26:41).

The first two verses of the psalm are a strong incitement for prayer. The psalmist is addressing his soul when he says: "Praise the Lord, O my soul"; not once, but so many times as to be continuous. Throughout all of our days, praise and glorify the Lord. Your whole life must be a praise to, a hymn to, and a glorification of, God.

The soul must become a harp which praises in hymns the glories and benefactions of God. From childhood into the depths of old age, until the last breath, "Praise the Lord, O my soul."

Yes, "I will chant unto my God for as long as I have my being." This verse, according to an ancient interpreter, has deep meaning. It means that the glorification of God will not last only till death, but because the true man is the soul and this soul continues to exist beyond the grave, the glorification will not stop with the death of the body, but will continue into the other life, into infinite ages, and in fact the souls of the righteous shall see the grandeur and magnificence of God in a new light and shall praise Him together in hymns with the angels and archangels. Their chief work will be the praise and glorification of God.

Two things impel man to glorify God. One is God's omnipotence. The other is God's love for man. Let us make some more observations on the interpretation of this psalm.

God's power! O the power of God! Most people forget that above all is the omnipotent God, and for this reason become devoted and adhere to people who either have money or hold a high office. Many gather around the rich and famous people, the political and military officials, the kings and governors. There are also cases where the majority of people place their hopes in public officials, and those officials are honored and venerated like gods. While some powerful political or military official is praised and glorified by all mouths, God is completely forgotten.

An example from China demonstrates this. In this vast country one man succeeded in grasping all the political and military power. The people bowed down to him and worshipped him like God. His followers maintained that from even his thoughts, every good thing flowed. He is not living anymore. But when he lived, a terrible earthquake took place in China and millions of people had to evacuate the cities and villages in the area. What did their leader do, whom they deified? Absolutely nothing. And like common mortals, he trembled with the others.

The power of the leaders of the earth is small — very small, unimportant and temporary. Today, they live and threaten the world; tomorrow, they die, or fall from high places, are thrown into jails and become the derision of the world. That is why the psalmist says: "Trust ye not in princes, in the sons of men in whom there is no salvation. Do not put your trust in the leaders of the world who themselves are men, and do not have the power to save you."

Where must we base our hopes? In the omnipotent God. The God whose power is vast, unlimited and invincible. Take a look at the heavens, at the earth, at the seas, and see all that God has created; admire and glorify His power.

Along with God's omnipotence you must admire and praise His love of man, his benevolence! It is an unfathomable ocean. Here in a few verses are the psalmist's vivid descriptions of God's love towards men. "The Lord defends the wronged. He gives food to all those who hunger. He frees the imprisoned and enslaved; he opens the eyes of the blind; He sets up and supports the fallen. He loves the righteous. He protects the strangers who do not have families and friends. He protects the orphan and the widow. He disperses the cunning schemes of the enemy. The Lord lives and reigns unto the ages." Therefore praise the Lord, O my soul. "I will praise The Lord in my life, I will chant unto my God for as long as I have my being."

What a pity a psalm like this is not chanted every time the Divine Liturgy is celebrated!

WHO DIDST DEIGN

We spoke in our previous homily about the second antiphon, the 145th Psalm. Let us continuously prompt ourselves, saying "Praise the Lord, O my soul. I will praise the Lord in my life, I will chant unto my God for as long as I have my being."

While this psalm is being chanted, the priest in the holy bema is saying the prayer: "O Lord, our God, save Thy people and bless Thine inheritance; protect the whole body of Thy Church and sanctify those who love the beauty of Thy house. Do Thou endow them with Thy divine Power and forsake not us who have set our hope in Thee."

This prayer of the second antiphon is a beautiful prayer of the Church. It contains many divine meanings and needs further examination. But because this prayer is repeated at the end of the Divine Liturgy, we will speak about it, with God's help, in the second part of the explanation, when it will be heard again.

Immediately after the cantor chants: "O Son of God, Who didst rise from the dead, save us who sing to Thee: Alleluia," he chants: "Glory to the Father and to the Son and to the Holy Spirit. Both now and ever and unto ages of ages. Amen." This hymn is a short doxology to the Triune God. Glory to the Father, glory to the Son, glory to the Holy Spirit. Glory unto ages of ages. We spoke about this doxology to the Holy Trinity in a previous homily.

After this doxology, the following hymn is chanted: "O Only-begotten Son and Logos of God Who being immortal, yet didst deign for our salvation to be incarnated through our Holy Lady and Ever-Virgin Mary, and without change didst become man and wast crucified, by death overcoming death, do Thou, Christ our God, save us; Thou Who art One of the Holy Trinity and art glorified with the Father and the Holy Spirit." This hymn speaks about Christ. In a few words, an answer is given to the question of who Christ is and what His work on earth was.

Let us try to examine the meanings of this wonderful hymn, which is a brief statement of the mystery of divine dispensation. Christ is not a creature. He is not like the sun, the stars, the angels and archangels, and man. He is God. He is the second person of the Holy Trinity. He is the Only- begotten Son. He was begotten by the Father not in the way in which everyone else is begotten, but in a unique way. Because, according to the first meaning, a child which is begotten by a father is chronologically subsequent. But Christ as the Son of God is not chronologically subsequent, but is coeternal with the Father. This St. John the Evangelist proclaims at the beginning of his Gospel: "In the beginning was the Word, and the Word was with God and the Word was God" (John 1:1). Namely, the Father always existed and the Son always existed.

This truth of the faith is emphasized because in the ancient days there were, and even today there are, heretics saying that Christ did not exist from the beginning together with the Father, but that He came into existence afterwards. They say there was a time when the Son of God did not exist. To that, the hymn responds, saying: "No, Christ existed, exists and will exist always. His existence is eternal. Human reason cannot fathom in what sense Christ, the Son of God, was begotten of the Father. And I ask you: Is this the only mystery the human mind cannot understand? Nature is full of mysteries, and scientists, in spite of all their efforts, cannot explain them. And when even material things which are in front of our eyes enclose in themselves mysteries, then how do we have the capacity to understand the infinite mystery which the Deity contains? We must kneel with humility before this infinite mystery and say :"Who is so great a God as our God? Thou art the God who worketh wonders" (Psalm 76:14-15). The only God.

O Holy Trinity: Father, Son and Holy Spirit, have mercy on us. Being full of egotism we seek to explain the unexplainable, and are in danger of falling into errors, as did Arius and other heretics – and more recently the so-called Jehovah's Witnesses – and might lose our soul. O Holy Trinity, make our faith like a rock so that it cannot be shaken by any satanic power.

The first truth which this hymn proclaims is that Christ is the Only- begotten Son and Logos of God. The other truth is that the Only-begotten Son and Logos of God received flesh from the Virgin Mary, became man and as man walked on earth, associated with men and accepted death on the cross, vanquished death, and ascended into Heaven and is glorified with the Father and the Holy Spirit.

Unfortunately, these truths make no impression on many of us. Let us pay special attention to the word *"katadexamenos"* (Who didst deign) of this hymn, used by the hymnographer to explain the mystery of the incarnation of God. The meaning is: Christ, Thou Who art above all creatures, the King of the angels and arch-angels, the Creator and Molder of all the universe, Thou didst deign to become man in order to save us. O Christ, who can describe the height of Thy majesty and the depth of Thy humiliation, Thine infinite love for us men?

"Thou Who didst deign." When we people hear that some great and powerful man of today went to spend a few moments with some poor unfortunate person living in a hut, we consider it something great and wonderful. But what is this compared to that which God has done: descended from the heights of Heaven and visited men?

Alas! We praise and admire the small things. The greatest, we don't even wonder at and believe. However, Justinian, one of the greatest emperors of Byzantium, marvelled at this. And to honor and glorify Christ, not only did he build the Church of the Holy Wisdom (Haghia Sophia) at Constantinople, but he also wrote this wonderful hymn: "O Only-begotten Son and Logos of God...," which we hear at every Divine Liturgy.

THE BEATITUDES

In my preceding sermon, we interpreted that marvelous hymn, "O Only- begotten Son and Logos of God." We said that this hymn is a poem which was written by the pious Byzantine emperor Justinian. This hymn, as we said, is a short statement of the mystery of Divine Providence, of the Incarnation. It declares what the Creed declares about Christ. It is a confession of faith that was incorporated into the Liturgy of the Catechumens, because the Catechumens in the Early Church used to leave after the reading of the Gospel and did not remain to hear the Creed. Thus, with this hymn, the Catechumens hear and proclaim their faith in the Triune God. In other words, this hymn is the "pre- Creed."

Beloved, it is plain that everything that is said in the Divine Liturgy has its place and is not said without purpose.

And now, let us proceed to the Divine Liturgy. After the hymn "O Only- begotten Son," the priest once again says the short petition: "Again, yet again in peace let us pray to the Lord...." At the end of this petition, he makes the exclamation, "For Thou, O God, are good and lovest mankind and to Thee we ascribe glory, to the Father and to the Son and to the Holy Spirit, now and ever and unto ages and ages. Amen."

After this exclamation, the cantors chant, or should chant, the Third Antiphon, which consists of the Beatitudes (Matt. 5:3-12).

We shall devote a few words to the Beatitudes. We say a few, because he who undertakes to interpret and explicate the contents of the Beatitudes, will not reach all the depth of the divine meaning, no matter how great an interpreter and theologian he is.

The Beatitudes are the beginning of a sermon which Christ gave while on a mountain, where many people had gathered. For this reason this sermon is called "The Sermon on the Mount." It is the longest of Christ's sermons and it is preserved in the Gospels (Matt. chapters 5-7; Luke 6:20-49). The sermon begins with the word "Blessed" [The Greek word for "blessed," *makarios*, was translated into Latin as *"beatus."* Hence the name "Beatitudes"].

Christ uses that word nine times. The repetition of that word shows the worth of the ideas and things which Christ recommends as necessary for a person's happiness.

"Blessed." This word means a person who has found happiness. But while all people seek happiness, they are not in agreement as to what makes them happy. There are different ideas and perceptions about this question.

If you take a survey and ask who ought to be called a happy person, you will receive various answers: Happy are the rich. Happy are the shipping tycoons. Happy are the rulers and leaders. Happy are the carousers. Happy are those who possess and receive material goods. Happy are those who have as their motto: "Eat, drink, and be merry, for tomorrow we die" (cf. I Cor. 15:32). Happy are the scientists. Happy are....

This is the language of the world. This was also the language of men at the time when Christ was living.

Everyone, both great and small, considered the man who succeeded in gathering and enjoying material goods, in acquiring wealth, power, glory and honors, to be happy. The language of contemporary people who believe in materialistic theories, rather than in Christianity, does not differ from the vocabulary of the ancient Epicureans and other early materialists. A certain modern so-called philosopher created out of his imagination an individual who would succeed in gathering all of the power, crushing all others in his path, and who would place his throne on top of the ruins of other people. He named this person of violence, of cruelty, of inhumanity, "Superman" *(ubermensch)*. Happy is the superman!

In His Beatitudes, our Lord Jesus Christ overthrows the ideas and things which men bless. He takes the ideas and things which people despise and makes them the foundations of a new state of ideas and things, of an ideal society, of the Kingdom of Heaven. In Christ's Beatitudes, it is not wealth, nor glory, nor power, nor transient pleasures and enjoyments, which are blessed, but instead goodness and virtue. Yes, virtue. Not the virtue of the scribes and the Pharisees; not the virtue of the philosophers, of proud and egotistical people; not the virtue which boasts of outward deeds; but the virtue that has its root in the inner man, in the mind and heart of a person.

Happy are those who have knowledge and consciousness of their imperfection, weakness and sinfulness. These are the *humble*. These are the ones who follow the maxim "Know thyself." Some people, when they hear the first beatitude, "Blessed are the poor in the spirit...," think that this is a blessing of the feeble-minded, of imbeciles, of idiots. This is a terrible misinterpretation of the meaning of the first beatitude. Not stupidity and idiocy, but *meekness* is blessed. Meekness is higher knowledge, true wisdom and understanding. Haughtiness and egotism are forms of stupidity and idiocy.

Blessed are those who are humble. *Blessed* are those who are sorry and grieved by the evil which exists in the world and which makes people distressed. *Blessed* are those who hunger and thirst after righteousness. *Blessed* are those who have a pure heart, cleansed of faults and evil. *Blessed* are those who contribute to the predominance of God's peace on earth. *Blessed* are those who suffer afflictions and persecutions while preaching the Gospel.

And who do we think became the first blessed person? Some great and powerful person, one of the scribes and Pharisees? No. The thief who repented on the cross became the first blessed person. He became conscious of his lowliness, repented of his wretchedness, showed meekness, proclaimed the truth, and sought God's mercy. He truly showed himself to be blessed. For this reason, before the Beatitudes are chanted, the verse "Remember me, Lord, when Thou comest into Thy Kingdom" (Luke 23:42), is chanted.

COMMON PRAYERS

Beloved, the old practice of the Church was to chant the Beatitudes before the Small Entrance of the Gospel in the Divine Liturgy. As we have said, the Beatitudes of the Lord were the Third Antiphon. In our previous sermon, we described the meaning of the Beatitudes. Those who have the virtues which the Gospel recommends are truly blessed, happy and fortunate. But unfortunate are those who have vices and passions, which like wild beasts have their dens in the depraved heart. The pure heart of the faithful person is a small paradise. But the heart of a faithless and depraved person is a miniature hell.

While the cantors chant the Beatitudes, the priest stands with great reverence before the Altar and says the following beautiful prayer:

"O Thou Who hast given us grace at this time with one accord to make our common supplications unto Thee and dost promise, that when two or three are gathered together in Thy Name, Thou wilt grant their requests: fulfill now, O Lord, the petitions of Thy servants, as may be the most expedient for them; granting us in this world knowledge of Thy Truth, and in the world to come life everlasting."

The interpretation is as follows: "Here, O Lord, where we gathered together and are celebrating the Divine Liturgy and are addressing our prayer to Thee and are asking Thee for all of our material and spiritual needs; we are following Thy Commandment. For Thou hast said, O Lord, 'Where two or three people gather in My Name, I will also be there among them.' And here in this holy temple where we are gathered together, more than three in number, for the sake of Thy Holy Name, and not for any other purpose, we feel Thy presence and, relying on Thy promise, we are certain that Thou wilt give us what we are asking for if it is in accordance with Thy Will. Therefore, we ask for knowledge of Thy Truth and eternal life."

Let us examine somewhat the meanings which this prayer of the Third Antiphon contains.

"Common prayers." This means prayers which one does not say while alone in one's room, but rather prayers in which two, or three, or more people participate, they are joined by the same faith in the true God, in the Triune God, joined together by the sweet Name of Christ. The presence of the Lord becomes strongly perceptible in the holy fellowship which common prayer creates. One feels this when one finds oneself in a typical congregation, one consisting of zealous Christians who truly believe and who participate in the Divine Liturgy with deep humility and holy contrition. Common prayer, the attendance at church by the faithful, their participation in public worship, is no small matter.

"Where there are two or three gathered together in my name, I am there with them" (Matt. 18:20). This is the promise which Christ made not only to his first disciples, but also to Christians of all times. St. John Chrysostom, while speaking about this subject and explaining what a source of divine blessings the gathering of Christians is, relates the following example: "Suppose that you are outside the borders of your country in a very distant land where a different language is spoken and where the people seem very strange to you. Imagine your distress in the foreign land, a land that is not only strange, but which is also inhabited by people with barbarous, pagan customs. You walk along the roadway distressed and sorrowful. You cry and sigh. Suddenly, you hear someone speaking your language, the language of your homeland. Imagine the joy you will feel at that moment! You will draw near to that person, greet him, kiss him like a brother. And by conversing with this person, you will be relieved of the heaviness in your heart which is caused by your being in a foreign country. The name of your homeland ties you together."

Fellow-Christian, you can understand the deeper meaning of the words of Christ from this example which St. John Chrysostom relates. "Where there are two or three gathered together in my name, I am there with them." Christians (and when we say "Christians" we do not mean just nominal Christians but rather those who believe sincerely in Christ and struggle to live their lives here on earth in accordance with His holy will), conscious Christians, are always very few in number in this world. The other people who do not believe in Christ and are cold and indifferent do not want to have anything to do with a faithful Christian, even if they are neighbors, friends, or relatives. They speak sarcastically of him, they mock him, curse him, slander him, and calumniate against him.

The true Christian, who loves the Lord and follows His divine commandments, feels like a foreigner. Others do not understand his language. They speak another language, the language of self-interest, of advantage, of pride, the language of the devil. In this world, the Christian suffers psychologically. It is as if he were living in a foreign, barbaric, and pagan land (and what is even worse, if we really think about it, no idolater in the ancient barbarous pagan lands insulted his false gods). But here, in our so-called Christian country, a day does not pass (what am I saying – an hour does not pass) within which so-called Christians do not blaspheme the sweet name of Christ. For this reason, the Christian, the true Christian, is very glad to meet another person who believes in and loves Christ and has the same views and feelings. He is happier than the sojourner in a foreign land who meets a compatriot. But where else will one find brother Christians except in the environment of the Church?

Common prayer, I repeat, is no small matter. Let others praise the *Common Market* which will bring happiness to our unfortunate Land. We want to praise *common prayer*, the meeting of Christians everywhere, but especially in church, as being a source of divine blessings for the individual, for the family, for our nation.

Through common prayer many astonishing miracles occur. A certain saint said: A prayer said by many people together spreads light so that one may realize his mistakes. It gives strength so that one may reform them. It creates kindness so that one can forgive, and warmth so that one can dedicate oneself, so that one can love God and one's neighbor. The power of common prayer will make the Gospel alive, and the Kingdom of Heaven a peaceful and blessed reality.

KNOWLEDGE OF THE TRUTH-EVERLASTING LIFE

Beloved, the preceding sermon was about common prayer. We said what common prayer is. But many people today do not pay any attention to the subject of common prayer. They work together, they eat together, amuse themselves together, but they never pray together. For them, common prayer is something unknown.

In the old times, however, when faith was strong, Christians who would encounter each other would begin and end their meeting with fervent prayer, thanking God for their meeting and asking Him to help them in whatever they had need. Common prayer brought them together spiritually, and their love and solidarity were amazing.

However, even today, in this age of unbelief and corruption, there are examples of Christians who pray together. There is a doctor, one of the best in Athens, faithful and dedicated to the Lord. When he visits patients and sees that their condition is serious, he kneels by their bedside and prays to God, together with the patients and their relatives. Patients experience a unique feeling of consolation and power after this common prayer. But this Christian doctor from Athens is unusual. One seldom finds others like him in Greece. However, people who have been sick and who have gone abroad for treatment, and have been hospitalized in the great hospitals of Europe and America, say that often doctors and nurses pray with their patients, creating a religious atmosphere with their prayers. Christ, the true God, who is the Physician of souls and bodies, makes His presence felt in these situations of common prayer. When will we see the common prayer of doctors and patients in our clinics and hospitals?

But Christ's presence is stronger and more perceptible when Christians are gathered together in the holy places of churches and celebrating the Divine Liturgy and praying together. "Lord, we thank Thee," the priest says in the prayer of the Third Antiphon, "we thank Thee for common prayer . . .. And now that we are gathered together, we ask with humbleness for 'knowledge of Thy Truth and eternal life in the age to come!' "

Let us explore in this sermon what "knowledge of the Truth" and "everlasting life" mean.

Knowledge! By "knowledge" we mean not just general knowledge, but rather exact knowledge of a thing.

People see many things. But an uneducated and casual observer sees things differently from a scientist who examines and investigates things from every angle. For example, what is a tree? Everyone sees trees, but what is a tree? How does it begin from a seed? How does it develop? How does it breathe? How does it blossom and bear fruit? An agriculturist gives much thought to these and other questions about the life of a tree. Despite all of this research, none of the agriculturists can say that he has an exact knowledge of trees. As scientists examine and research the various topics of their field, they progress in their science, in their knowledge of matters.

People today show a great deal of interest in finding out as much as possible about events and phenomena in Nature. Their curiosity reaches the point where they seek to discover the elements of which the other planets are made. They seek more knowledge, precise knowledge about all things. They want to learn the truth and be informed. But (strange to say), while people of our time show so much interest in learning about the things of this world, they are so unconcerned and indifferent about the things of God, the things of faith. If you ask them how many Gospels there are, or how many epistles the Apostle Paul wrote; or how many psalms David wrote; or what the prophecies of Isaiah and Jeremiah are; or who the great men and events of the Old and New Testaments were; if you ask them about any of these things, they will not give you a right answer. These people do not have knowledge of the truth of God. Since they are ignorant of the True God, of His Holy Will as it is expressed in Holy Scriptures, they live in spiritual darkness, they fall into errors and heresies and commit terrible sins and crimes, as the Apostle Paul describes in the first chapter of his Epistle to the Romans.

In contrast, the pious Christian has a great desire to learn the Gospel. And for this reason, he does not limit himself to listening to the Gospel and the Epistles once a week, but rather tries to budget time every day to read one or more chapters from the Holy Scriptures. He examines and dives into the meanings of the Scriptures. He feels that to understand the truth of the Gospel, it is not sufficient simply to read the Scriptures, but that it is most important for him also to pray and to ask for enlightenment from God, so that he can learn the Truth. He does this because a person's heart will remain a locked prison, if the Holy Spirit does not open it. Being closed from all sides, the sun's rays are not allowed to enter from anywhere. The key with which the Christian opens the Scriptures and by which he will come to know the greatness of God is prayer.

Therefore, one thing which we ask for in the prayer is knowledge of truth. The other is blissful life in the age to come.

Life in the age to come! What do we, the people of the twentieth century, the age of deceit, we who have our gazes fixed on the here-and-now, have to say about eternal life? This life attracts us and we tremble lest it escape our hands. We tremble at the realization that death comes and cuts the thread of this life.

No reasonable person can deny that life on earth is precious. It has its charms. There are so many beautiful things in nature that one can hardly think of them all. There are the green valleys, the fruit-bearing trees, the forests with their dark shade, the springs with sparkling waters, the rivers, the lakes, the high snow-capped mountains, the fathomlessness of the ocean, the chirping birds, the sheep which graze in the green meadows, the countless fishes, the cool breeze, the sun which gives heat and light. Each and every one of these divine creations evokes admiration, and gives an exquisite beauty to the face of the earth.

But beloved, if life here on earth is beautiful, imagine how much more beautiful, pleasant, and charming, eternal life will be! It is the life which begins after the grave, in another world which God has created for man. And that world is called Paradise.

O Lord, we ask You to open our eyes so that we can know Thy greatness and enjoy Thy glory! Together with the priest, we pray in common prayer and say: "Give us 'the knowledge of Thy Truth and eternal life in the age to come.' "

THE ALL-HOLY VIRGIN AND THE CHILD CHRIST

III

THE
SMALL ENTRANCE

THE SMALL ENTRANCE

Beloved, the Divine Liturgy proceeds. The priest at the Holy Altar prepares for the Small Entrance after the prayer of the Third Antiphon. In this sermon, we shall see what he says during the Small Entrance and what the Small Entrance is.

As we said previously, the Divine Liturgy is a wonderful panorama. It is as if an astonishing film, presenting different scenes of the life of Christ, were being unrolled before our eyes.

In the beginning, petitions, psalms, and hymns are heard. They reach a crescendo with a voice that comes from the aching heart of wretched humanity: people seeking salvation, but not finding this salvation anywhere. One after another, all of those who acted as if they were great, and presented themselves as saviors, and promised to deliver the world from its suffering, accomplished nothing. And wretched mankind despaired.

From the midst of the wretched world, from the depths of every heart which felt the evil pressing like a mountain and creating agony, there would come a voice of supplication to heaven. It would beg God to pity the sinful world and to send a Savior and Redeemer. And this voice of every sinner and of every afflicted person is heard intensely at the beginning of the Divine Liturgy. It reaches a crescendo when the hymn, "Save us, O Son of God...," is chanted.

And the Savior, of whom the Prophets of old prophesied and for whom mankind awaited with longing, came. Christ came. He was born at night in a cave in Bethlehem. The angels sang, "Glory to God in the highest, peace on earth, goodwill to men" (Luke 2:14). "Glory to Thee Who hast shown (us) the light," chants the Church, hailing the dawn, the sweet daybreak of that holy and mystical day. Christ has come.

The Divine Liturgy is a copy of Christ's life. Christ was born in Bethlehem, baptized in the Jordan River, tempted in the desert, entered public life, preached His gospel, performed miracles, walked to Golgotha, offered His precious blood, was buried, arose, and ascended into Heaven. All of this awesome mystery of Divine Providence appears in the Divine Liturgy.

Seeing the Divine Liturgy from this perspective, the Small Entrance is the appearance of Christ into the world as a teacher. The Great Entrance is Christ's journey to Golgotha, the performance of the Highest Sacrifice.

The pious congregation has prepared itself with doxologies, prayers, psalms, and hymns to receive Christ as the Teacher and Preacher of Truth. When the holy moment of the Small Entrance arrives, the celebrant priest bows and kisses the Holy Gospel with great reverence, as the cantors outside, in the nave, chant the Apolytikion of the day. He holds it with highest devotion and raises it with both of his hands, makes a left turn around the Holy Table, and exists through the north gate of the sanctuary.

An altar boy ("a little priest," as we in Greece say today), holding a candle, goes before the priest. The commentators say that this candle, which goes before the

Holy Gospel, represents John the Baptist, the Forerunner, who appeared like a lamp, like the morning star, and announced the coming of the Sun, Christ. All just and holy people who lived before Christ in the terrible pagan darkness used to shine, as stars shine during the night. The saints are stars, and St. John the Baptist is a star of the first magnitude, a morning star. But the Sun which warms and casts light upon everyone's heart is Christ. He is the Sun which will never set. Glory to Thee, O Christ, Who hast shown (us) the light!

The faithful, upon seeing the priest holding the Holy Gospel and proceeding to the main section of the church, stand up if they are seated, step down if they are in the stalls, bow, and make the sign of the cross. The chanters also must show their reverence and come down from the choir platform. Christ is coming to teach us, to preach His truth. The Teacher and Professor, the only one Who is worthy to be called "teacher" and "professor" in the absolute sense, is coming.

Christians listen to the voice of the Church which is inviting them to receive Christ. "Come, let us worship and bow before Christ. Save us, O Son of God, Who didst rise from the dead. Save us who sing unto Thee, 'Alleluia.'"

Speaking about the Small Entrance, we must know that in the old days the Gospel was not placed on the Holy Table. It was kept with the holy vessels in a special place in the church called vestry (*skevophylakion*, lit., "place for guarding vessels"). From there the priest would take the Gospel and transfer it to the Holy Table in a procession whenever the Liturgy was celebrated. This official transfer of the Gospel was called "the Small Entrance."

We must also know that in the old days, before the invention of the printing press, the Gospel was a book written by hand on parchments, of elaborately prepared animal skins, and hence it was a very expensive book. Only the rich could afford to have a Gospel in their homes. This is also shown by the life of St. John the Hut-dweller. This saint came from a wealthy family and asked his parents to give him a Book of the Gospels as a gift, while he was still young. Hearing their child's desire, his parents bought him one, which he kept with him all of his life up to his death. From this Book, his parents recognized him a few hours before he died.

Such Gospels, written with fine handwriting on parchments by the hallowed hands of monks and illustrated with beautiful icons, still exist in the monasteries of Mount Athos. They are precious heirlooms. They are worth millions. A century ago, one such Gospel Book was stolen by a visitor at the holy monastery of Sinai who sold it to Czarist Russia for a million roubles. It was sold by today's atheist Russian leaders to the British museum for millions of pounds.

But let us take heed, beloved. The value of the Gospel does not lie in its being covered with gold and silver and precious stones. By no means. Its value is intrinsic. Its value lies in the immortal words which it contains. These words have greater value than all of the gold of the world.

Today, the Book of the Gospels, which formerly was the property of few people, is, with the invention of paper and printing, an inexpensive book. Even a very poor person can afford to buy one. In this way the Book of the Gospels may be found not only in monasteries but also in many homes, both those of the rich and those of the poor. It can be read by the great and the little in all of the world. My fellow Christians, I ask you: Do you have a Book of the Gospels? If you do not, buy one and read it every day.

ANGELS AND ARCHANGELS CELEBRATE WITH US

We are at the Small Entrance. Following what we said before, the priest, holding the Holy Gospel, stands before the Beautiful Gate, bows his head reverently, and says:

"O Master and Lord, our God, Who hast constituted the orders and armies of Angels and Archangels to do the service of Thy glory in Heaven, grant that there be with our entry, an Entry of Holy Angels, serving with us and with us glorifying Thee for Thy Goodness. For to Thee belong all glory, honour and worship, to the Father and to the Son and to the Holy Spirit, now and for ever and from all ages to all ages. Amen."

This prayer mentions angels and archangels who take part in the Divine Liturgy, praising and glorifying God.

This century of materialism and disbelief has shaken the faith of many, and they question belief in angels and archangels. In fact, a certain unbeliever of our time who flew a rocket into outer space, said sarcastically at his return that he met no angels anywhere out there. What arrogance and ignorance these words display! Humanity has gone but a little distance away from the earth, like going a single step outside the yard of one's house, and it thinks it has seen everything. Yes, one step into space and, right away, he was filled with pride and thought he had seen the whole universe.

Yet, the universe is so large, so vast, that scientists say that man must travel not months or years, but millions of years – at the speed of light! – to reach the ends of the material universe or the more remote celestial bodies.

But more significantly, what such a person did not take into account was that the material world is not the only one that exists. Holy Scripture, the immortal Book, tells us that another universe exists beyond the material – the spiritual universe. There we find angels and archangels, that is to say, beings who do not have bodies like our own. They are therefore called incorporeal, immaterial. Being free of a gross body, they move about easily, and like messengers and faithful instruments of God, they carry heavenly messages and execute divine orders. Their primary function is to glorify God.

Being God's creation, angels and archangels were created before the stars, as is implied by a passage in the Book of Job. There it says that when God created the countless suns and stars, and light shone everywhere, the angels stood amazed at the splendor of such a divine creation, and they gave God praise and glory (Job:38:7)

Also, in the Book of Isaiah the Prophet, there is a wonderful image of Divine splendor as the prophet saw it. The Prophet saw a throne, higher than any other throne. On this throne he saw seated "the high and exalted One," the Lord. He saw the House of God. He saw it radiant with Divine glory. Around the throne he saw angels and archangels. He saw Seraphim, each one of these spiritual beings having six wings. With two wings they covered their faces, with the other two, their feet, and with the third two they flew. They cried to one another, spoke in one divine accord, and a wonderful hymn was heard: "Holy, holy, holy is the Lord of Hosts; the whole earth is full of His glory" (Isaiah 6).

Another prophet, Daniel, also described God's glory. He said that God, the "Ancient of Days, Who is outside time, the eternal and immortal One, sat on the throne. And the throne was like a "flame of fire" and "its wheels were a burning fire." And a river, not of water, but of fire, flowed before Him, and countless spirits, angels and archangels, were serving the Lord (Daniel 7).

The same army of holy angels and archangels which surrounds the throne of God, to praise and glorify Him, came down to earth on that unforgetable night when Christ was born in a cave at Bethlehem. The Evangelist Luke says "a great army of heaven's Angels" was praising God, saying, "Glory to God in the highest, and on earth peace, good will toward men" (Luke 2:13-14).

Angels, these bodiless, immortal spirits, come down and fill the church, and celebrate along with the priest of the Most High God during the Divine Liturgy – even if the church is a deserted mountain chapel.

What great and high things these are to understand! Angels in heaven, and on earth as well. Angels in church, where the Divine Liturgy is celebrated and the awesome Mystery of the Holy Eucharist is offered. With the King of Glory are also the angels and archangels, His faithful servants, the untiring singers of divine splendor.

Angels and archangels at the Divine Liturgy of Orthodox Christians? This you should believe and sense during the Divine Liturgy. And if you are a saint, like St. Spyridon, you will not only feel them, but see them, too. St Spyridon had such awe and contrition, that when he celebrated the Liturgy, angels and archangels would appear next to him, and chant the divine hymns. This is stated clearly in his Apolytikion: "Divinely inspired Spyridon, our father,... when reciting thy holy prayers, thou didst have Angels to assist thee. Glory to Him who, through thee, gives healing to us all!" Do you hear what the Apolytikion say? You, St. Spyridon, when celebrating the Divine Liturgy, had not only other priests as co-celebrants, but angels and archangels as well.

O Christ, who dost love the Church above all else, Thou didst shed Thy precious blood to save humanity. We pray to Thee, give to Thy Church priests and bishops like St. Spyridon, who will celebrate Thy Divine Liturgy with awe and contrition. Then Thy deserted churches will be filled once more with congregations of faithful souls!

According to the prayer of the Small Entrance, the Divine Liturgy is a celebration of human beings and angels together, surrounding the throne of the Most High, chanting Alleluia.

Priests of the Most High God! Christians, whom God allows to come to church! Pray to the Lord to give us contrition, so that we may feel and live the splendor of God in the Divine Liturgy.

SUPREME WISDOM

"Wisdom! Let us arise!"

We continue the explanation of the Divine Liturgy. We are at the Small Entrance. We said that the priest takes the Gospel Book from the Holy Table, goes out the North Door of the church, stands before the beautiful Gate, says the silent prayer which we explained, and, lifting the Gospel Book, says, "Wisdom! Let us arise!"

What does this exclamation mean? Please listen to this short and simple explanation. All Christians hear "Wisdom! Let us arise," but few understand this important exclamation, and even fewer live and feel the reality which these words represent.

First of all, what is wisdom? Wisdom is thought to be knowledge. But wisdom is not simply the knowledge one gets through observation of things that exist. It is also knowledge which is not satisfied by a simple explanation of a certain thing, but proceeds to learn the "how" and "why" – the secrets which everything, even the smallest of things, hide. And the smallest thing is that which science calls the atom.

Though the atom cannot get any smaller, and is much smaller than the point of a pin, it still contains a mystery, a hidden power; and science, after much research and experimentation, succeeded in splitting the atom, and from this fission came energy, an enormous power we call nuclear power.

The scientists who worked and discovered nuclear power are admired the world over and are called wise, because they saw with the eyes of science things which, for thousands of years, people could not see.

Wisdom, therefore, is knowledge, scientific knowledge.

Science examines and investigates material things, and quite often makes discoveries without, of course, succeeding in permanently solving the problems of the material world. It solves one problem, only to be faced with another.

But beyond the material world there is the spiritual. There we find people's thoughts, feelings and wills. There we find the spirit. There is the invisible soul, which thinks, feels, and does the most daring and terrifying things. There we find life beyond the grave. There, hell and paradise. There, angels and archangels, and above all these is God. It is certainly easy for us to say that none of these exist, and that the only thing that exists is matter. Denial is easy! But the problems which result from denial of this sort are such that, into the life of the most avid unbeliever and atheist, there come moments which shake him up, and he asks, "Is there only matter?..."

The ancient philosophers occupied themselves with questions about the spiritual world. They attempted to find the beginning and the end of all things; but they erred in their explanations of spiritual and invisible things, and deceived themselves, and their deception reached such a point that reciting the foolishness of these old philosophers provokes laughter. For example, one thought that the souls of the dead became the little insects born in fava beans, and so this philosopher ordered his followers not to each fava beans! Others taught similar follies. So, humanity was forced to live in ignorance of the great and high problems of life; and it did not involve little, trivial things, like a handful of soil or piece of stone, but questions upon which their eternal fate depended.

With regard to the great questions, humanity wandered for centuries; for thousands of years it was in deep darkness, and could find no exit.

You may have heard of the labyrinth. Whoever entered this labyrinth to see what was in it wandered through its many dark corridors and could not find the way out. They say only Theseus was able to enter the labyrinth and come out again, using a thread.

The ancient world was like the labyrinth. The philosophers, trying by their own knowledge to answer the great questions of life, wandered through the chaos of various philosophic ideas and systems, and kept the world in darkness. St. Paul said that they were proven foolish: "They say that they are wise, but they are fools" (Romans 1:22).

Christ's teaching, the Gospel, brought the world out of the labyrinth of sin and error. Yes! The Gospel is true wisdom in divine matters. It is truth and life. When I was serving in Florina as a preacher in 1942, a blessed boy who shined shoes wrote the following words on his box:" The Gospel is the highest philosophy of life." I asked him why he wrote those words, and he answered that, from the moment he took the Gospel in his hands and read it, he felt that everybody in the world has a value, and this filled his heart with joy.

People from all parts of the world, who once lived in the dreadful darkness of error and sin, have picked up and read the Gospel. A brilliant sun has begun to shine in their hearts, and they have thanked God for this great gift.

Dear friends, the Book of Gospels is incomparably superior to every other book in the world. It is the King of Books.

That is why the priest during the Small Entrance raises the Book of the Gospels so that everyone may see it, and says: "Wisdom!" That is to say, the book I am holding in my hands is wisdom. Whatever it preaches is the truth. And because Christ continues to teach the whole world with this Gospel, the entire congregation should stand to welcome it, honoring and giving thanks to Christ.

That is why the priest, after the exclamation "Wisdom! Let us arise!" chants: "Come, let us worship and bow unto Christ. O Son of God, who didst rise from the dead, save us who sing unto Thee: Alleluia."

THE HYMNS

The priest, after chanting the hymn "Come let us worship...," enters the sanctuary through the Beautiful Gate and places the Bible on the Holy Table.

Immediately, three or four hymns are chanted alternately, that is, one by the priest, the other by the cantor. The first hymn which is chanted is the Apolytikion or dismissal hymn of the day.

The Resurrection Apolytikia of the eight modes or tones are: of the first tone, "When the stone had been sealed...;" of the second, "When Thou, the deathless life, didst come down to death...;" of the third, "Let the heavens rejoice...;" of the fourth, "The women disciples of the Lord learned from the angel...; of the first plagal tone, "Let us the faithful praise and worship the Logos...;" of the second plagal, "The angelic powers...;" of the grave tone, "Thou hast destroyed death by Thy cross...;" and of the fourth plagal, "From on high Thou didst descend...." And these eight Apolytikia speak of the glorious Resurrection of Christ. The Resurrection of Christ is the miracle of miracles; and belief in Christ's Resurrection is a cardinal doctrine of the Church.

On Sunday, one of the Resurrection Apolytikia is chanted. If the Divine Liturgy is not celebrated on a Sunday but on a weekday, then the Apolytikion of the feast day is chanted after the Small Entrance. If a saint is commemorated, the Apolytikion of the saint is chanted. If the All-Holy Virgin is commemorated, then the Apolytikion of the feast of the Theotokos is chanted.

After the Apolytikion of the day, and that of the saint who's being commemorated, the Apolytikion of the saint of the church is chanted, and lastly the Kontakion (such as: "O protection of the Christians...").

These three or four hymns which are chanted after the raising of the Bible give a special character to the Divine Liturgy. (The term "raising" is used here because the Bible is always carried in a raised-up position by the priest to denote its holiness and honored position in the Church). They indicate the name of the church and the day on which the Liturgy is celebrated.

And now a question: Why was it ordained that these hymns be chanted after the Small Entrance?

The interpretation of a contemporary student of the Divine Liturgy, Gervasios Paraskevopoulos of blessed memory (the term: of "blessed memory" denotes some pious individual who passed away), come to mind, and we answer as follows:

There are people who, when they hear about the Bible, say that those things which the Bible preaches are beautiful and great teachings, but... who follows them? They say, namely, that the teachings of the Bible are inapplicable, that the Bible is beautiful theory which no one is able to practice. And since the Bible cannot be practiced, other teachings, more practical, more contemporary, must be heard and used. The Bible then is useless, they say; various other teachings of the world are useful and beneficial, according to such people, even though such teachings are very often put into circulation by the devil in order to deceive people!

Such people are in error. The Bible *is* applicable. It can be applied by everybody at all times and in all places. Proof of this lies in the saints, whose memory is celebrated and whose Apolytikia are chanted. Every day the Church puts before us one or more saints. And these saints are not only monks who left the world and went to the mountains and deserts, and there spent their lives in fasting and prayer. If only these people who left the world and hid themselves in caves became saints, St. John Chrysostom says, the Gospel would appear to be written only for ascetics. Do not show me only monks and ascetics to prove that the Gospel is applicable, says the holy father. Show me a man who does not live in the mountains but lives in the midst of society and has a wife and children and labors and works and fights against many obstacles and temptations, and though he lives in the world, under so many adverse conditions, is not stopped from applying the Gospel to his life. This man who lives in the world and who lives the Gospel is a great proof that the Gospel is applicable and that it has the power to create a new society of people.

In the *Life of Saint Anthony*, who was one of the great ascetics of the desert, we learn that at one time he was tempted by pride. The thought came to him that he was the most holy man in the world. But immediately he heard a voice which said to him: "Anthony, you're mistaken. The most holy man is in another place...." And the angel (for it was an angel who had spoken to him) offered to show him where this holy man was. He led him to Alexandria, and there, in a poor neighborhood, he showed him the saint. He was a poor head of a family, and, in spite of his economic troubles, gave alms and helped those who were poorer than himself.

If we open the book *Lives of the Saints (Synaxaristes)*, we will see that there were saints who were farmers, shepherds, craftsmen, teachers, professors, scientists, and inventors. Saints from all professions, saints from every age group, saints from all countries and all peoples and all languages. Saints not only of ancient times, but of contemporary times. Saints even in our own age. Yes! In the midst of the terrible filth of human society, God has hidden His diamonds; He has His saints: men, women, and children.

And all these saints, these noble beings, contradict with their lives those who say that the Gospel is inapplicable. It was applied in ancient times. It is applicable also today. It will be applicable always. Those who follow it may be few. But these few are enough to prove that the Gospel gives birth to heroes and martyrs, who are the noblest children of the earth.

For this reason, the Divine Liturgy presents the saints, chants their Apolytikia, honoring and extolling them, so that we might imitate their example, as they imitated the example of Christ and lived in accordance with the Bible.

Η ΦΙΛΟΞΕΝΙΑ
ΤΫ ΑΒΡΑΑΜ

THE HOSPITALITY OF ABRAHAM

IV

THE THRICE
HOLY HYMN

THE THRICE-HOLY HYMN

"Holy God, Holy Mighty, Holy Immortal,
have mercy upon us."

We continue our interpretation of the Divine Liturgy. The hymns which are chanted following the Small Entrance, and we hear the exclamation of the priest: "For Thou our God art holy, and to Thee we ascribe glory, to the Father and to the Son and to the Holy Spirit, now and ever, unto ages of ages." The Thrice-Holy hymn is then chanted: "Holy God, Holy Mighty, Holy Immortal, have mercy upon us."

This hymn has great importance for the Church. A historian of Byzantium, Theophanes, mentions the following event concerning this hymn. When Proclos (433 A.D.), a student of St. John Chrysostom, was Patriarch of Constantinople, the city was shaken by earthquakes continuously for four months. The inhabitants, terrified, ran outside the walls of the city to a place called Campoi, and there prayed, and with tears in their eyes asked God to stop the earthquakes. One day, when the earth was trembling and the people were crying, "Lord have mercy," an unseen power carried off a child from the midst of the people, raising him towards heaven. And when the child came back to earth, he said that he heard a divine voice which ordered him to tell the bishop that intercessions must be chanted as follows: "Holy God, Holy Mighty, Holy Immortal, have mercy upon us." Patriarch Proclos ordered that this hymn be chanted. And when they began chanting it, the earthquakes stopped.

With prayer, with the "Holy God...", the earthquakes stopped. Perhaps someone who is educated, and boasts of his science, will laugh upon hearing this, and say: "What's this you're saying to us? An earthquake is a natural phenomenon and has nothing to do with God...." But the word of God assures us that earthquakes and all the other natural phenomena which take place in the world are dependent on God's power. The psalm says: "Who looketh on the earth and maketh it tremble, Who toucheth the mountains and they smoke (103.35)." St. John Chrysostom says that the cause of earthquakes is God's wrath, and the cause of God's wrath is the sins which people do continuously, young and old, clergy and laity.

The faithful, therefore, chanted the "Holy God..." with great contrition during the terrible earthquake of Constantinople, and the miracle took place. We also chant this hymn today in church. It is chanted by fine voiced chanters who try with all their skill to chant beautifully in order to gratify the people. He who can prolong his chanting for a very long time is considered a chanter of renown. But we ask: What is the spiritual benefit of this? Does God listen to these voices? Does He become merciful of our sins because of this chanting? It is possible that because of these ostentations of the chanters, and the lack of piety and contrition of us all, we sin in the church and provoke God's anger. Alas! How far we, contemporary Christians, are from the worship of God "in spirit and truth" (John 4,23).

There is a need to return to the piety of our ancestors. We must return to the ways of ancient times, when

Christians chanted the Thrice-Holy Hymn with tears in their eyes. For when the Christian is taught, and knows what is meant by all that is said and takes place in the Divine Liturgy, there is the hope that this Chirstian shall feel the grandeur of sacred worship.

Let us therefore see briefly what the Thrice-Holy Hymn means.

"Holy God." We spoke about the Saints in previous homilies. But by comparison with God, what is even the most holy man? One drop in comparison with an endless ocean. One ray in comparison with the sun. God only is holy in an absolute degree; God is the source of holiness and sanctification. Man is enlightened by God and receives the power (from God) in order to live a life of holiness, which no matter what great heights it reaches, is small and unimportant in comparison with the infinite holiness of God. No one is holy like God.

"Holy Mighty." Power is another attribute of God. Man is also called mighty. But man's power, no matter how great it is, no matter what mighty things he can do — even if he flies to the stars of the heavens — is small and unimportant in comparison with the all-mightiness of God. The Lord of power is God. From Him comes every power and energy in the world. As a certain poet says, "One of God's looks has the power to shake the earth;" it is possible for the universe to dissolve into the elements "from which it was made" and a new world to be created.

"Holy Immortal." Another attribute of God is immortality. God is immortal. What does immortality mean? While all things waste away and are destroyed, God remains unaltered, imperishable, eternal, immortal. He is life. He is the source of life. And if man is immortal, he is immortal not because of himself, not, that is to say, because of his own power, but because God created him "according to His image and likeness" and gave him the gift of immortality. Man is immortal in soul, perishable in body, because of sin. But this perishable body shall become imperishable and eternal in the kingdom of heaven.

In the Thrice-Holy Hymn, the word Holy is repeated three times. This threefold repetition is done purposely to show the three Persons of God, that great mystery of our faith that God is three Hypostases (or Persons). We worship and glorify one Divinity in three Persons. These three Persons – the Father, the Son, and the Holy Spirit – are one Divinity. That's why we do not say in the Thrice-Holy Hymn: "You (plural) have mercy on us," but "have Thou (singular) mercy on us."* The three attributes we have mentioned – holiness, mightiness, and immortality – are attributes of the Father, of the Son, and of the Holy Spirit. As Father, as Son, as Holy Spirit, O Holy Trinity, glory to Thee!

My dear readers! We have seen the miracle that took place in Constantinople. We have seen the meaning of the Thrice-Holy Hymn. Priests, chanters, and laity: let us be careful during the time of the Thrice-Holy Hymn, and let us pray to the Triune God with pious contrition and a spirit of humility.

---

*In the Greek, from which we translate this, the author uses a plural construction which cannot be directly reproduced in English, except by indication: you (plural), and thou (singular). In the Thrice-Holy Hymn as given to the Church by this miraculous occurrence, the thou form is used, and definitely has a singular character.

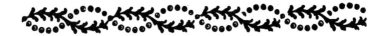

WHERE GOD REPOSES

While the Thrice-Holy Hymn is chanted, beloved, the celebrant priest stands in front of the Holy Table and says the following prayer, which is called the prayer of the Thrice-Holy Hymn. This prayer is one of the most marvelous prayers of our Church, and reads as follows:

"O Holy God, Who restest among Thy saints and art glorified by the Cherubim and praised by the Seraphim with thrice-holy voice, and worshipped by all of the Host of Heaven; Thou Who hast brought all things out of nothingness into being; Thou Who hast created man in Thine image and likeness, and hast adorned him with all Thy favors; Thou Who givest to the suppliant wisdom and prudence and dost not neglect the sinner, but hast accounted us, Thy humble and unworthy servants, worthy to stand at this time before the glory of Thy Holy Altar and to bring to Thee meet adoration and praise; do Thou, Master, accept, even from the mouth of us sinners, the Thrice-Holy Hymn and visit us in Thy Righteousness; forgive us all our transgressions, voluntary and involuntary; sanctify our souls and bodies and grant that we may worship Thee in holiness all the days of our life; through the intercessions of Thy Holy Mother and all the Saints, who from the beginning of time have pleased Thee; for Thou, our God, art Holy and to Thee we ascribe glory, to the Father and to the Son and to the Holy Spirit, now and forever and unto Ages of Ages. Amen."

Let us try to explain the meaning of this prayer.

The priest confesses at the beginning of the prayer that God is the Holy One. That is to say, He has holiness from Himself to an absolute degree. He is, as we said, the source of holiness and of sanctification. Being holy, He rests and dwells in pure hearts that love Him and are dedicated to Him. St. Basil the Great, speaking on this subject in one of his homilies, in order to show how much God loves purity of heart, gives as an example the bee. The bee, he says, goes only to the flowers that smell sweetly. From them it takes whatever it needs to make its precious honey. Therefore, as the bee likes the flowers that are fragrant, in the same way God, the Holy Spirit, is pleased to visit and remain in hearts which are pure, and by His grace makes the sweet honey of virtue. The pure heart becomes God's house, God's dwelling place, the temple of the All-Holy Spirit. The Psalmist proclaims the same thing when he says: "Create in me a clean heart, O God, and renew a right spirit within me" (Psalm 50, 10).

The prayer continues: "God, Who is holy and Who is worshipped by multitudes of holy angels and archangels, by the cherubim and seraphim, created the universe out of nothing."

"But can anything be created out of nothing?" asks the man who tries to unravel everything with his mind alone. If it seems unbelievable that out of nothing God created the universe, how much more unbelievable is it for someone to say the whole universe came into being without God? As you see, unbelief, instead of unraveling the problem of the world's existence, makes it more difficult. For who can ever believe in atheism, which states that all things that we see came into being by themselves? The world is not something insignificant and accidental. It is made with such wisdom, even in the tiniest things, that the sincere scientist who studies and examines them is forced to marvel and proclaim the existence of the omnipotent and all-wise God, and repeat David's words: "How magnificent are Thy works, O Lord! In wisdom hast Thou made them all" (Psalm 103,24). Even one ray of the sun, one drop of water, one leaf of a tree, one feather of a bird, one seed, one handful of soil – what am I saying? – even the tiniest thing called an atom, is enough to prove that there is a God. Without the existence of God the universe remains an insoluble enigma.

But even if all that we see on earth and in the sky were not there, and only man existed, he alone would be enough to prove that there is a God. What is man? Man is not only a body, he is not only that which is seen, but is also that which is not seen. And that which is not seen is chiefly man. It is his spirit. It is reason and free will, those two great gifts, that testify that man has a higher destiny than all of material creation, and that he is related spiritually to God. He was created "according to the image and likeness" (Gen. 1, 26) of God. This also the Thrice-Holy Hymn avows.

Man the image of God? Man, who tells lies, slanders, and defames the innocent; who steals, deceives and forges; wallows in the muck of dishonorable passions; takes a knife and kills his fellow man, and opens his foul mouth and blasphemes his Creator; this man then, who commits so many indecencies, infamies, and crimes, who surpasses wild beasts in ferocity, is an image of God? Many might ask us this question.

We answer: Man's moral state is truly lamentable. It makes us recall the God-inspired words of David: "And man, being in honour, did not understand; he is compared to the mindless cattle, and is become like unto them" (Psalm, 48, 13, 21). Man, that is, who did not appreciate the exceptional place God gave him in creation, fell and became like the animals.

However, in spite of corruption, man preserves in the depths of his being traces of his moral origin. God's image was not destroyed. "It was distorted," as the Fathers of the Church say. And to give an example: In ancient Byzantine churches there are excellent mosaics, which represent Christ and different saints. When the Turks conquered our land, they made the churches into mosques and plastered over the beautiful mosaics, in order that they might not be seen. However, the mosaic icons still existed, though covered. And as the churches again become Christian, we remove the covering, clean the icons, and again they appear in their original splendor. Such a thing happens with the soul of man, the image of God. Sins covered and dirtied the image. But the image was not lost. Grace comes, washes the image, and it appears more splendid. Man is renewed by the power of God.

The Triune God was marvelous, therefore, when He created man "according to His image and likeness." But much more marvelous is God when He renovates sinful man, makes him new again in His divine workshop, which is called the Church.

These meanings, and many other still are contained in the wonderful prayer of the Thrice-Holy Hymn.

HE IS COMING . . .

"Blessed is he who comes in the name of the Lord."

We find ourselves, beloved, at the Thrice-Holy Hymn. While it is chanted, the celebrant priest with great reverence stands in front of the Holy Table, turns to his left, towards the place of the holy offertory, bows his head, and says: "Blessed is he who comes in the name of the Lord." Now what do these words mean? And why does the celebrant turn towards the place of the offertory?

"Blessed is he who comes..." is a hymn which the Hebrews chanted (Psalm 117,26). They chanted it in ancient times, before Christ, when they welcomed high personages, glorious generals and kings, who returned as victors from wars. But they chanted it too at the time of Christ.

In the beginning, as we know, the Hebrews did not pay any attention to the person of Christ. They saw Him as a poor man Who worked in Joseph's workshop, cutting and carving, making doors and windows, and in this way, with His labor, earning His daily bread. Christ as a poor worker! Who could imagine that in this poor and unimportant man was hidden all of Divinity? Others in His time shone in the eyes of the world, a world that measured — and continues to measure — the value of a man from his outer appearance and things, from wealth and honors, money and glory. Dung covered with gold-dust! Such were, and are, the grandeurs of this world.

Christ was a poor and unimportant worker. But when He came out into His public life and started to preach words that were never before heard, and to perform miracles that were never before seen, the world began to pay attention to Him. Every day Christ acquired greater validity. The people, comparing Christ with the Scribes and Pharisees, saw how much greater He was in wisdom, teaching, strength, and works. Before Christ all the wise and great waned like lamps before the sun. The Scribes and the Pharisees were little men with their little passions, while the virtue of Christ was like the sun, greater than the sun. Christ's virtue "covered the heavens."

The people marvelled at Christ. And their marvelling reached its zenith when shortly before He was crucified, after three years of public life, He went to a little village a short distance outside of Jerusalem, to His beloved Bethany, and there performed the greatest miracles of all that He had done until this time. He stood before a grave that hid a man four days dead, His friend Lazarus, and cried out: "Lazarus, come out!" At his command, death retreated, and Lazarus was resurrected (John 11, 1-44). Lazarus, for the remainder of his life, was a great proof of Christ's power.

The news of the resurrection of Lazarus spread everywhere by word of mouth. Like lightning it reached the capital, Jerusalem. This was the topic of the day. Everyone discussed and everyone marvelled at the power of Christ. Before Christ not only the Scribes and the Pharisees, but even the greatest men of the Old Testament, appeared small. Christ was greater than even Moses and David.

The Jewish people were a poor and scorned people that had lost its political and religious freedom and independence. They lived under Roman domination, and everyday saw the proud Roman soldiers, the legionaries, passing through the streets, and the Roman flag waving in Jerusalem. This tortured and despairing people saw hope in Christ. They saw Christ, and said: "He will liberate us from the Romans!" And because of this, when it was heard that Christ was coming from Bethany to Jerusalem, the people were electrified. Everyone, young and old, dropped every other topic and discussed Christ, and said: "He is coming!" And as it is written in the Bible, "When they heard that Jesus was coming to Jerusalem, they took branches of palm trees, and went forth to meet him and cried, 'Hosanna: Blessed is the King of Israel that cometh in the name of the Lord!' " (John 12, 12-13)

But Christ did not come for only one people, the Judaic people. He came for all the peoples of the world. He came to free man from slavery and tyranny. But which slavery and what tyranny? The worst kind: the kind that sin creates for man. For sinfulness is the most miserable and tyrannizing state. It is the most ancient "state," which gives birth to all the other hateful states. And as long as sin exists, people will suffer from all of the other bad states.

Christ came to destroy the domination of sin and to bestow to mankind the greatest and most beautiful freedom, the true freedom, for which mankind thirsted from the most ancient times, freedom from passion and guilt. That is why in the writings of the whole ancient world was heard a voice, saying: "He is coming, the redeemer of the world is coming!" The expectation of the redeemer was so strong that when America (which was cut off from the rest of the world for thousands of years,) was discovered, its people asked the first Europeans to set foot on their soil, with much feeling: "Has the Saviour of the world come?"

God be praised! The Saviour of the world came. He was born in Bethlehem of Judea. Peoples and nations, be glad and rejoice!

This event, the greatest event in history, when God became man and came to the world to save it; this event which, in the language of theology is called the Incarnation of the Logos of God; this event, from Nativity to the Crucifixion and the Resurrection, is reenacted in front of our eyes by the Divine Liturgy. And the "Blessed is he who comes in the name of the Lord" corresponds to the day of the triumphant entrance of Christ into Jerusalem, when countless people received Him with palms and cheers. In the same way, at this point in the Divine Liturgy, when the Thrice-Holy Hymn is chanted and we are ready in a little while to receive Christ "as the King of all," we repeat the jubilant verse: "Blessed is he who comes in the name of the Lord."

May this verse come out from the depths of our heart, so that we do not become like the Hebrews, who at first were shouting, "Blessed is he who comes," and after a few days were shouting, "Away with him, away with him, crucify him."

STRENGTH! *(DYNAMIS)*

In this homily, beloved readers, we will limit our discussion to one word only. "What?!" someone might say, "You are going to limit your sermon to just one word?" Yes, just one word!

There are in the world very small things, with great value. An example: diamonds are very small stones, but each one of them has more value than a mountain of rocks.

The same occurs in speech. There are words, thousands of words, which come out of the mouths of garrulous and foolish people, that all together do not give us one serious meaning. There are newspapers, magazines, and whole books which do not give one drop of substance when passed through the press of logic, and squeezed. But there are cases where a few words give an important message, make an impression, evoke emotion, and become a motivating force for a higher life or heroic decisions. All of us know from school the great significance of the two words that Leonidas spoke at the narrow pass of Thermopylae: *"Molon labe"* ("Come and take it"). It was the answer to the proud Persian invader, who wanted Greece to surrender. We all know also the great significance, not only for Greece but for the whole free world, of a small word that Greece said in 1940, through the mouth of its Premier, to the Italian dictator: "No!"

But if a few words, which are said on certain occasions, have such importance, then how much more important are the words of the holy books of our Church — especially the Holy Writ, and also the Divine Liturgy, (which contains the rich meanings of the Holy Writ). And a proof of this is the word *"Dynamis!"*, which is heard from the deacon, or from the priest, when there is no deacon. It is heard before the last repetition of the Thrice-Holy Hymn.

What does the word *"Dynamis"* (or, "Strength") mean? There are two interpretations. According to the first the word *"Dynamis"* is hortatory; it is a call to the chanters to chant the last repetition of the Thrice-Holy Hymn with a stronger voice.

"Dynamis!" ("Strength!") If we are attentive to the priest who celebrates, we will see how the tone of his voice is not the same during the entire liturgy. There are times when the priest is completely silent and says prayers inaudibly. There are other times when he says them in a low voice. Sometimes he raises his voice and says them loudly, "with great voice". There is also a time when the voice must be raised to the loudest level, and that is why the command: *"Dynamis!"* (or, "With strength!") is given.

Has this interpretation anything to teach us? Certainly it has much to teach us. There are many people who, when they hear a preacher raise his voice at one or more parts of his sermon, become upset and say that this should not be done. "A sermon," they say, "must be tranquil, the words like soft rain." But a sermon which is not simply the sermon of a preacher, but the voice of the Church itself, is the Divine Liturgy, which we hear every Sunday, or more often. Therefore, the Divine

Liturgy, that superb, unattainable sermon, must not be said in only one tone. The voice of the liturgist must be varied according to the directions of the Typicon (the directory of all church services and practices of the Church: or rubrics). Monotony is boring. The voice must vary in tone not only to avoid monotony, but also that some particular parts might be emphasized, and greater attention and feeling called to them. The commands in the army are not given with a soft voice, but with a strong one, so that the most lazy soldier is shaken out of his indolence and is attentive and becomes active. In the same way, the church, which is a camp of militant people who are called to fight in a spiritual fight, hears the strong voice of the liturgist. This wakes the attention and the interest of the slothful Christians.

"Dynamis!" ("Strength!") The voice does not always have the same intensity. God made the cords of the larynx, a marvelous instrument, so the voice might be low at one time, and high at another; baritone at one time, tenor or soprano at others. This variety helps a person to express with his voice the variety of his spiritual conditions. Watch a mother. Her voice is soft, quiet and caressing when she has her child in her arms, or when she wants it to sleep. If the child is in danger of having something happen to it, such as falling into the fire or falling down she raises her voice greatly. She cries out loudly, in order to bring it to its senses; and this strong voice of the mother saves the child. The same happens with the brooding hen. Her voice is softer when she calls her chicks to give them some seed or other eatable that she has found. But when she sees a hawk or a sinister bird in the sky ready to pounce, her voice becomes strong, and she calls her chicks to gather near her in order to cover them with her wings.

And Christ also, Who is the founder of our holy religion, and is our exemplar, did not always speak in the same tone — as we see in the Gospel. His voice had a different tone when he snapped the whip and chased off those who sold and bought in the temple, and made the house of God into a "house of commerce"; or when He censured the hypocritical Pharisees with those terrible "woes," which like thunderbolts fell on their heads (Matt. 10,27; John 2, 13-16; Matt. 23, 13-29). And when He was before large audiences and wanted to emphasize what He was saying, He raised His voice to be heard by all. The Gospel says it clearly. When He was in Jerusalem at Solomon's Temple during a great holy day, He cried out, "If any man thirst, let him come unto me, and drink" (John 7,37), which is to say, let him hear the heavenly teaching.

"Strength!" O chanters, you who will now chant the "Holy God" for the final time: raise your voices not to show-off, but to forcefully express your devotion to the Triune God. Tens of thousands of beautiful voiced chanters are not enough to praise the grandeur of the Triune god.

"Dynamis!" But besides this interpretation there is another one. This word, which is composed of three syllables, *'Dy-na-mis'*, is a summary and abbreviation of the Thrice-Holy Hymn, according to some. As it is changed in the hymns of Pentecost, "one power (*dynamis*), one expression, one worship of the Holy Trinity."

Dynamis! O Holy Trinity, have mercy on the world, and on us, the sinners.

THE VINEYARD OF GOD

Beloved, we are discussing the wonderful Thrice-Holy Hymn which we hear in the Divine Liturgy, and the other things said while that hymn is being chanted. Let me add the following by way of a final homily on this hymn, which one pious interpreter has named "The Hymn of Hymns to the Holy Trinity."

When a Bishop celebrates the Divine Liturgy, at the last "Holy God," he comes out of the Beautiful Gate while holding the *Dikerotrikera* (a triple candle in his right hand and a double candle in his left), and prays for the people with the following prayer, which he directs to God three times:

"O Lord, Lord, look down from heaven and see; have regard for this vine, the stock which Thy right hand planted" (Psalm 79:14-15).

First of all, let us see what the "Three-Candles-Two-Candles" means. The "Three-Candles" are bound together with a ribbon and held in a smaller holder with three apertures, one candle in each. These symbolize the Holy Trinity. The Father is Light, the Son is Light, the Holy Spirit is Light — the triune Divinity. An infinite and incomprehensible mystery! Seeing the three lights these candles give, our thoughts and hearts should be moved towards the triune God.

The "Two-Candles," which are bound and held in the other candleholder, symbolize the two natures of Christ.

Christ is both God and man, the God-Man. Divinity and humanity were united in one Person, the Person of our Lord, Jesus Christ. Seeing these two lights, the faithful Christian directs his mind and heart towards Christ, who is the Light of the world.

With these two sets of lights, then, which symbolize the mystery of the Holy Trinity and the mystery of the two natures of Christ, the Bishop appears at the Beautiful Gate. He turns first to the icon of Christ, then to the holy Theotokos; and at each of these positions he recites the prayer we mentioned above.

Let us try to give a short interpretation of this beautiful prayer.

The bishop asks the Lord to look upon our vineyard with love from the Heavenly heights, to visit it and help it grow, because it is His vineyard. It is the vineyard that He Himself has planted.

But someone may ask: "What vineyard?"

If we open the Old Testament, to the Book of Psalms in particular, we will see that the Hebrew nation was the first to be called a vineyard. The 79th Psalm says that this nation lived under the terrible slavery of the Egyptian kings. By a series of miracles, God took them out of this cruel bondage to Pharaoh, and planted them like a vineyard in another land, Palestine, having all the blessings of God. This vineyard took root in the Holy Land; it grew and spread over a great area and brought forth good fruit.

The Hebrew nation was the chosen vineyard of God in the ancient world. But unfortunately, this chosen vineyard, admired by all, was destroyed because of its sins. The select grapes it produced, virtue and goodness, disappeared, and great heroic deeds also vanished. The vineyard was destroyed. It fell as if prey to hail or locusts. It was as though wild swine had entered it, and had not only eaten the grapes and leaves, but had dug with their snouts to throw the roots of the vines into the air; and nothing remained.

The old vineyard had been destroyed, but God planted a new vineyard with His right hand. This vineyard is the Church that Christ established. Please open the Holy Scriptures, and read the 21st chapter of the Gospel according to St. Matthew, as well as the 15th chapter of the Gospel according to St. John.

The Church is the vineyard of Christ. But just as a real vineyard has more than one grapevine, one root, so the Church has many grapevines; that is to say, many people, men, women and children who are joined to Christ, the root, like grapevines, and from Christ they receive whatever they need for their spiritual life.

Christ loves His vineyard with Divine love. He waters it with the precious Blood He shed on the Cross, which is offered to the Christian each time the Divine Liturgy is celebrated. The Christain who is not watered by Christ's Blood will become a dry root. Christ is the life which feeds every grapevine, every Christian.

And if the Christian shows imperfections and faults, Christ — who cares for and watches over His whole vineyard, the whole Church — will not leave Christians to their imperfections. He desires their perfection, and like the vinegrower who prunes his vineyard with a pruning-hook, stripping it of useless twigs, Christ has His own pruning-hook. Christ's pruning hook is suffering the world's many sorrows. Every Christian is pruned by this holy pruning-hook, stripped of unnecessary and useless things, and is made stronger to produce rich fruit and good works.

Christ has also placed workers in His vineyard. They are obliged to watch over the vineyard and cultivate it according to His orders. The honorable workers of the vineyard are bishops and priests, basically,and when all these perform their duties as they should, then the vineyard, that is, the diocese or parish, will be a chosen vineyard which the angels will behold and rejoice.

The Church is God's vineyard. But, dear friends, we feel like crying, because the exceptional vineyard called the Orthodox Church no longer produces the rich harvest She produced in times past. What is worse, She seems barren and dry, as though a blight fell upon the vineyard; and as is the case with a blight, the leaves become yellow and fall off, the roots dry out, and the vineyard is spoiled. In the same way, lack of faith and great corruption this century have spoiled Christian communities. Of the countless grapevines which once existed, only a few continue to be joined to Christ and receive power through Him.

The vineyards have withered! Who is responsible? Mainly, the ones charged with protecting and cultivating the spiritual vines, the parishes and dioceses. O God, be merciful to the world, and to us, the clergymen of the 20th century!

"O Lord, Lord, look down from heaven and see; have regard for this vine, the stock which Thy right hand planted."

The Crucifixion

V

THE READINGS

SHINE . . .

Dear friends, the Divine Liturgy continues. The Thrice-Holy Hymn has ended. You can see movement in the Sanctuary. The altar boys, dressed in their robes, are getting ready; they light the candles which they will hold before the Gospel Book when it is brought out for reading. The priest is censing the Holy Sanctuary and the people, and before the Epistle and Gospel readings, the priest sends up the following prayer to God:

"O merciful Master, cause the pure light of Thy knowledge to shine in our hearts, and open the eyes of our mind to perceive Thy message of Good Tidings; fill us with the fear of Thy blessed commandments, that we, trampling down all fleshly desire, may seek a heavenly citizenship, and may do all those things that are well-pleasing to Thee. For Thou, Christ our God, art the Source of Light to our souls and bodies, and to Thee we ascribe glory, with Thine Eternal Father and Thine all-holy, righteous and life- giving Spirit, now and forever from all ages to all ages. Amen."

Let us try to explain this beautiful prayer.

To understand this prayer, let us open the New Testament and carefully read II Corinthians, chapter 4, verses 3-6. The Apostle Paul talks about darkness and light. He distinguishes between two kinds of darkness and light. The first darkness was the one which covered the universe before God created light, as the Old Testament states at the very beginning: "In the beginning, God made the heaven and the earth. But the earth was without form and void, and darkness was upon the face of the deep." But when God said: "Let there be light," then the darkness was dispersed, and everything was illumined (Gen. 1:1-3).

Aside from the natural darkness which covered the earth at the beginning, there was also another darkness — a spiritual one. Spiritual darkness did not exist in the beginning because man, whom God created, had spiritual light within himself. The mind God gave him was pure and clear, and he was able to tell the difference between good and evil, between obedience to God's will and rebellion against it. Obedience to God was life; disobedience, death. But when man, because of his inexperience, was deceived by that Great Deceiver of Old, the devil, then the spiritual light he had in himself began to darken. The sins of their descendants were added to the sin of the first man and woman, and the spiritual light became more and more obscure. In spite of the fact that human civilization made great technical progress building towers, pyramids and great cities, humanity was nearly blind to virtue and the ability to recognize and do what was good. Not only was humanity near blindness, but it was as if it had been placed at the edge of a deep chasm, not in daytime, but at midnight — and as if that were not enough, humanity had an enemy following it, pushing it ever closer to that chasm.

The world lived in the midst of this terrible darkness, a darkness like that which existed before the creation of light. But God, who said, "Let there be light; and there was light," and the universe became bright, again said, "Let there be light," and through our Lord Jesus Christ, His only- begotten Son, there shone a spiritual light, and humanity was illumined. Our Church chants this beautifully in the Apolytikion (Dismissal Hymn) for Christmas Day, saying that Christ's birth "rose upon the world as the light of knowledge," and Scripture says: "The people sitting in darknesss and shadow of death saw a great light" (Is. 9:2; Matt. 4:16). Mankind saw the true light, God Himself, who became man. Christ is the Spiritual Sun for mankind.

But if Christ is the Light, the Sun of humanity, why are so many people living in darkness? The Gospel gives the answer. Christ is not to blame for it; neither is His holy teaching, which is all light. The fault rests in the evil and corrupted will of man. It is the miserable ego of man that doesn't want to open its eyes to Christ for illumination. Such people are like those who suffer from eye-trouble and are bothered by strong light; they avoid it, staying in dark places. Such people suffer from cursed egotism, sickly in their spiritual sight. They hate and despise that rich and beneficial light, and live like moles in the darkness of sin. As Christ Himself said, the light came into the world, but men loved the darkness more than the light, because their works were evil. For everyone who does evil hates the light and will not come to the light, so as not to reveal his works (John 3:19-20).

A person who feels his sinfulness also feels the need to be enlightened by Christ. Without Christ's illumination, people remain in darkness, despite all their scientific knowledge. They do not know where they came from, where they are, or where they are going.

Beloved, I once met a man who read many books and pretended to be wise. He did not believe in God. One winter night he was in a forest and a pack of wolves surrounded him. He was able to climb a tree, but the wolves did not leave the tree. They waited. The man spent hours of unimaginable agony on that tree until daybreak, when the wolves left. There, on the tree, he remembered his sins, and made a fervent prayer to God. He cried. And ever since that time, he has believed in God, and every morning when he gets out of bed, he stands piously facing east, saying a prayer of his own: "O Christ, send me one ray of Thy light to illumine my heart." One ray of light is enough to illumine the darkness of man.

"O my Christ! Now, when Thy sacred and holy Gospel will be heard, send one ray and open the eyes of our souls, so we can understand Thy divine words. Plant the fear of Thee in our hearts to conquer our carnal desires, to think and do what Thou dost want us to do and to live a life truly Christian. Thou art the light. Thou dost warm our physical bodies with the bright light of the sun, and Thou dost illumine our souls with the bright light of Thy Gospel. O Christ, we thank Thee!"

THE EPISTLE READING

A few years ago, the Polychronion ("Many Years") of the King followed the Thrice-Holy Hymn. There were no Polychronia in the ancient Church. Christians used to pray to God for the kings and authorities who were their persecutors, that He might illumine them to become Christians, but there were no Polychronia.

They began chanting Polychronia when the persecutions ceased and Christian kings ascended the throne. Even then, Polychronia were not chanted at every Liturgy, but only on special occasions. In our country, however, the Polychronion was misused, and it scandalized people. We are not writing this now that the monarchy has been abandoned. When the kings were in their glory here in Greece, we boldly wrote that the Polychronion should not be chanted at every Liturgy. And we did not merely write. When a late king signed a decree favoring Freemasonry, we protested and stopped commemorating him. Today, unfortunately, when the political system is democratic, Freemasonry lives on, and many people in important places are Masons. As you can see, Masons thrive in every system.

The Polychronion is not sung in church at present. No one in civil authority is commemorated by name, and any priest or bishop who commemorates the particular name of an official who happens to be in church does not do well. It is flattery, which has no place in a sacred house of worship.

The Polychronion is no longer used, but another Polychronion is still chanted. It is the Polychronion, the *pheme* of the celebrating bishop. This is an old custom. It would be best if we limited these hymns, or even completely eliminated the *Many Years to the Master*. The ideal of a Christian life is not length of years, but holiness and work for the glory of God. A few years full of virtue and activity are more valuable than many fruitless ones.

Following the *pheme* of the bishop, the sacred readings take place. In the ancient Church, portions of the Old Testament were read. Remnants of this tradition remain in the *Prokeimena*, the psalm verses intoned before the reading of the Epistle. Examples of *Prokeimena* are the verses, "How magnified are Thy works, O Lord! In wisdom hast Thou made them all. Bless the Lord, O my soul" (Psalm 103:26, 1).

The *Apostolos*, as we mentioned elsewhere, is a book of our Church. It contains not only the sayings and facts about Christ's Apostles, but parts of their Apostolic teachings and work. It contains sections from the Acts of the Apostles, the Epistles of the Apostle Paul, and other Apostles: Peter, James and John.

Many churches' *Apostolos* is beautifully bound in silver or gold, as is the Book of the Gospels. The priest keeps it in the holy Sanctuary until it is time for the reading; then he presents it to the reader, who in turn makes a pious bow, takes it from the Priest's hands, and begins reading the selection for the day. The Epistle reading changes every day.

The Epistle reading is not a chant, it is a reading. However, many cantors do not read it, but chant it as if it were a hymn. When they chant it slowly, the words and phrases are not clear and the congregation cannot understand anything. But if the cantor is a pious man who has read the Epistle many times at home, and if the reading is heard clearly, the congregation, even if they cannot understand all of it, do understand a greater part of it and are benefitted. An Epistle reading, read clearly, is much like a sermon. Only at the end of the reading should the cantor read the selection with any kind of melody.

When the Epistle is read, Christians should listen; that is why the priest calls: "Let us attend!" from the Beautiful Gate before the beginning of the reading. He is saying; "Let us pay attention, brethren, to what the Epistle has to say to us today."

"Let us attend!" Because the Apostle we hear is not an ordinary person, whose words mean nothing or are of no importance. The Apostles are people whom our Lord Jesus Christ chose and sent to preach the true Faith to the world. If a messenger from one of the world's very powerful nations were to come to our country, everyone would listen to him attentively, would respect and honor him. So we should pay much more attention to those whom Christ once sent into the world to teach the truth. Christ said to the Apostles: "As my Father sent me, so also I send my disciples into the world. And whoever listens to them, listens to Me, and whoever despises their words, despises Mine" (John 20:21; Luke 10:16).

Most of the selections of the *Apostolos* are taken from the epistles of the Apostle Paul. When we listen to them reverently, it is like having St. Paul present before us. It is like seeing him with the eyes of our souls, like having him visit the big cities of our country once again: Athens, Thessaloniki, Corinth, Verroia, Philippi, Crete, Epiros, and to speak to us, the 20th-century Christians, with his divinely inspired words. The Apostle Paul is the mouthpiece of Christ.

"Let us attend!" Let us pay attention! What a sin we commit when the Epistle is read and our minds and hearts do not attend to the divinely-inspired words. Lord, have mercy on us!

THE GOSPEL READING

At the Divine Liturgy, we hear the voices of the Prophets in the Antiphons and *Prokeimena;*, we hear the voices of the Apostles in the daily Epistle reading; and in the Gospel reading we hear the voice of the Lord Jesus Christ. And because Christ, as God, is above all the Prophets, Patriarchs, Apostles, Angels and Archangels, the priest alerts the people when the Gospel is about to be read and prepares them, saying: "Wisdom; Stand and attend. Let us hear the Holy Gospel. Peace be with you."

"Gospel" is an English word used in ancient times to mean "good, happy news"; and because the interests and the psychological condition of people differ, the news that motivates them is also different. There are many different kinds of good news.For example, someone buys a lottery ticket. When the drawing takes place, he is informed that the number on his ticket wins first price, worth millions. His joy is indescribable. The news that his ticket has won is not small or unimportant; it is good news which pleases him. Someone else is imprisoned in a dark, wet jail. He suffers much. He awaits the time of his release. Unexpectedly, someone comes bringing news that the Governor of the State pardons him. The message is good news, which gladdens the convict. And yet a third person is sick. He has been crippled for months, having contracted a terrible disease, for which there is no treatment. Unexpectedly, however, he hears news on the radio that a cure for his illness has been discovered, and all those suffering will be helped. Can you imagine the joy of this sick man? The news for this sick man, news that a cure was discovered, is indeed good news.

There are many other kinds of good news. But of all the good news ever possible, one piece of good news is far better than all the rest. It is that Gospel which was heard one unforgettable night in one corner of the world, and thereafter spread throughout the whole world. It is the Gospel which the Angel of the Lord gave to the shepherds: "Do not be afraid! For I am here with good news for you, which will bring great joy to all people. This very night in David's city, your Savior was born — Christ the Lord!" (Luke 2:10-11).

This heavenly message that Christ was born, the Salvation of the world, means that whoever believes will be saved. They will be redeemed from the worst disease in the world, the disease no wise man or scientist can cure. The germs of this disease spread everywhere to cause physical and spiritual ruin and great calamity. This universal illness is sin.

Yes! Sin is the worst illness in the world. Unfortunately, most people pay no attention to it. They are not afraid of it. If only we sinners could understand what sin is, what its disastrous effects are even in earthly life, we could moan and, horrified, we would run without delay to Christ, the Savior of the world, to be cured, and to find spiritual health and salvation! The medicine is faith; faith in His Gospel, faith in the Blood which Christ shed on the Cross, which "makes us clean of every sin" (I John 1:7).

The Gospel contains heavenly news. The four Evangelists — Matthew, Mark, Luke and John — describe the life of Christ, present His teachings, and narrate His miracles. Certainly, they did not write everything Christ said and did. If everything were written down, as was once said, the sky should become paper and the sea, ink. But those things which the Evangelists wrote down present an excellent, untouchable image of spiritual greatness, the image of our Lord, Jesus Christ. This image was impossible for the lowly fishermen of Galilee to dream up; they saw it alive in the person of Christ, and were astonished. And this astonishment is also experienced today by all those who study the Gospels impartially. Undoubtedly, no other man ever said or did what Christ said and did.

Having such content, the Gospel is the Book of books, the King of the books. The influence it has had on the world has been enormous. Having committed horrible crimes and in despair of the world, sinful men upon reading the Gospel have found the right way, the way of salvation. They would not exchange the Gospel for any other book, any knowledge or treasure. Uncivilized people who used to eat their fellow man as if they were beasts, having read the Gospel and believed in it, changed completely. They became men of true nobility and virtue. Seeing such a primitive man, a Christian, reading the Gospel, a European asked sarcastically, "What?! Do you believe in this book?..." The primitive looked at him and asnwered: "If I didn't believe in this Gospel, I would have killed and eaten you by now...."

Yes! The Gospel is God's power for everyone who believes.

Because the gospel is so priceless, no one should be seated when it is being read. Everyone must be standing. Even the bishop, when he celebrates, removes his Omophorion, stands in front of the Beautiful Gate, and listens to the Gospel with the rest of the people.

But the Divine Liturgy is not the only place the Gospel should be heard. We should read it everyday. Let a day pass without bread, but not without the Gospel. "Wisdom! Let us stand!"

SACRED PREACHING

Following the Gospel reading is the sermon. Sacred preaching is teaching based on the written word of God, Holy Scripture, or a teaching which discusses the meaning of Holy Writ, teaching lessons to Christians.

There are those who do not want to hear sermons. They say that the Divine Liturgy, the sacred services, and the holy Mysteries are enough. They consider preaching an innovation introduced by Protestants, who have nearly abolished worship, and give preaching the highest place.

These people, however, are mistaken. Preaching is not an innovation, it is not something new; there has always been preaching. We could say that the history of preaching begins with the history of Church. We see this is the New Testament. We notice that when Christ began His public life, the first thing He did was preach. He began preaching by inviting people to repentance (Matt. 4:17; Mark 1, 15). He preached everywhere. He preached in the synagogues, where the Israelites use to gather to worship God. There, after reading the Old Testament text, He used to interpret what the Prophets said. And the people listened to His teaching with admiration.

Preaching was the first and foremost of Christ's tasks, and He commanded His Apostles to go into all the world and preach the Gospel. The Apostles' first sermon was the one given by the Apostle Peter (Acts 2:14-36) on the

Day of Pentecost. As we see in the Book of Acts, after the descent of the Holy Spirit, Peter, inspired by the Spirit, preached with frankness, courage and great power to thousands in Jerusalem, the center of Judaism. On the day Christ was judged, Peter denied Christ to a servant girl. He did this out of fear; but now he feared no one. The impression this first sermon produced was astonishing. Three thousand souls believed in Christ, and those three thousand established the first Church. Thus, the founding of the first Church of Christ was a result of preaching.

Preaching, however, did not stop at Jerusalem. The Apostle Peter and the others continued, particularly the Apostle Paul. They preached the Gospel wherever they went, and those Jews and pagans who heard it and believed formed the nuclei of the first churches.

Not one Church was established without sacred preaching, and no Church thrived or multiplied its membership without preaching. In subterranean cemeteries called catacombs, where Christians took refuge in times of persecution, there was always a sermon when the Divine Liturgy was offered. It was a simple preaching which came from the heart of the bishop or priest.

After the persecutions had ceased, and Christians came out of the catacombs and offered the Divine Liturgy in beautiful churches, there were still sermons. The preaching in the time of persecution had been short and simple, but now it took the form of rhetorical speech, and was systematized. It did not, however, neglect the depth and essence of Christianity. Great fathers and teachers of the Church excelled in this form of preaching. Words in the mouths of these holy teachers and homilists became a blazing sword to strike every heresy and error, letting the Church emerge victorious.

The Church, therefore, cannot be understood without divine preaching. It has great value. A more recent teacher of our Church, speaking about preaching, said that the rabbit is not as afraid of lightning as much as the devil is afraid of preaching. And another recent teacher of the Gospel, interpreting the Divine Liturgy, said that the entire history of the Church is a continuous chain of spiritual events created by preaching the word of God, united by Divine grace. The Fathers and Teachers, he states, are what Christianity has to show the world; the word and way of life. "In the beginning was the Logos, and through the word, the Logos will become the ruler of all."

Even the enemies of our faith – against their will – confess the value of preaching. When they attain power and become the leaders of their countries, of all religious doings, they fight the hardest against the word of God. They do not want Scripture readings. They do not want religious instruction. And they use pressure to have the Divine Liturgy celebrated without a sermon, because they know what influence the word of God has on souls.

For sacred preaching to have results, the Gospel's preacher must be the right person; that is, the Gospel preacher must have unshaken faith, and an ardent love of both God and sinful man. Next, he must live an unblemished life; for, if the preacher of the Gospel does not live by God's commandments, but acts contrary to the Gospel, the people who hear him will be scandalized and say: "Teacher, you teach but don't keep the Law yourself." Thirdly, the preacher of the Gospel must have knowledge of Holy Scripture, the sacred Canons and the Traditions of the Orthodox Church. Therefore, he must continuously study the sacred texts, and other religious books.

Effective preaching was always difficult, but it is especially so in our times. It is not easy for a person who lives in a faithless and corrupt generation to believe in the Gospel preaching. Preaching the word of God has to be as perfect as possible, and God's grace is especially needed.

Preaching is the main task of the bishop; but priests, deacons, and even pious laymen may preach. There are many examples of lay theologians who excelled in preaching the Gospel.

Christian friends, the bishop who writes these words believes in the Word of God, for it is God's power, and he does not cease preaching the Word of God both orally and in writing. Because it is not possible for him to be present in all parishes, he writes these meditations, so they can be read in every parish. In this way the lack of oral preaching by a bishop is somewhat filled.

THE RESURRECTION

VI

THE *EKTENES*
AND THE PRAYER
FOR THE CATECHUMENS

WITH OUR WHOLE SOUL

After the Gospel reading and the sermon, the priest sends up another series of petitions to God. This new chain of petitions is called an *Eketnes*. It is called such not only because it has many petitions and is extended (from the Greek *ekteino*, extend), but also because these petitions should not be said in a simple manner or blandly, but with sustained warmth. Today, unfortunately, these petitions are omitted due to lack of time. However, I believe that if cantors were to chant in a quicker tempo and did not take so much time with their lengthly *Dynamis*, there would be time for these petitions. Even now, there are pious priests who do not omit these beautiful prayers.

The *Ektenes* begins: "Let us all say, with our whole soul and our whole mind, let us all say...." But what does "with our whole soul and our whole mind" mean? We will try to explain this in our liturgical homily.

Let us begin with an example from our country's ancient history. In the third century B.C., a famous mathematician, Archimedes, lived in Sicily of Italy. Archimedes was very devoted to his science. His mind was occupied day and night with solving complex problems. He solved many, and we admire his wisdom to this day. He was so occupied with his science that once, when the city he lived in was besieged by Romans, and Roman soldiers conquered the garrison and advanced to the city's center, Archimedes did not stop his scientific work even at this fearful time. He had drawn circles in the sand and was attempting to solve a problem. A Roman soldier found him in this position, raised his sword, and beheaded him. Archimedes was so engrossed in his work that when approached by the soldier, he only turned his head and said to the soldier this famous line: "Please don't disturb my circles." That, my friends, is devotion, scientific devotion.

Not only Archimedes, but also many other illustrious scientists and philosophers give us examples of their devotion to the search for truth. They say that the renowned scientist Edison, who invented the electric light, was so devoted in his effort to discover something new that while working in his laboratory, he missed his own wedding ceremony! And, they say, the great ancient philosopher, Socrates, when he had a great idea and wanted to contemplate and meditate on it, would stand like a statue − even in the middle of the street − and would not move from that spot, having his mind fixed on the philosophic problem which engrossed him.

These examples, and many more, teach us what devotion means. It is an interpretation of what "with our whole soul and our whole mind" means. That is, just as the scientists and philosophers we mentioned had their minds fixed on their research, and would not allow them to drift to anything else, we should behave likewise when in the church. When we hear the sacred words and see the great Mystery taking place, we should not let our minds wander, running here and there, but we should concentrate completely on what is being said and done in the Divine Liturgy.

Christ, the crucified Redeemer, is the Alpha and Omega of our faith. He is hope and love. He is the axle, the center of the Divine Liturgy. Our minds should focus on the Redeemer, our hearts should love Him, our wills should incline towards Him, our whole being should be devoted to Him. There should be nothing else except Christ. We should say and do whatever He commands. Therefore, we should do that which the deacon or priest invites us to do at the beginning of this Extended Prayer.

Unfortunately, few of us attending church heed this invitation. As we said once before, we are in church only physically. However, even this is something significant, as St. Chrysostom said: "We do not deny it, because if we were not in church, we would be somewhere else, and who knows what sins we would be committing...." The nave of the church demands devoutness. It is not enough to participate in the Divine Liturgy physically; we must also participate spiritually. We should ask ourselves if we believe in Christ, if we believe He is God and Redeemer of the world, the greatest benefactor of humanity, to whom we owe not only our lives, but also our redemption from sin and death. If we do, then we should love him, not half-heartedly, but with our whole mind and heart. In church during the Divine Liturgy, our minds must be fixed on the great Mystery, especially at the most sacred moments. We will then be participating not only physically in the Liturgy, but spiritually as well. If we let our minds wander here and there, we will be there in body, certainly, but absent in spirit. We will not be worshipping our Lord "in spirit and truth" (John 4:23).

I will add another example to make my point clear. Our immortal soul, an excellent creation of God, when possessing a pure mind, noble feelings, and a good will, is a kind of divine palace, with many storeys and compartments. Christ, the King of All, is meant to dwell in this divine palace. But how many souls are suitable to become the bright residence of Christ? Unfortunately, instead of being Sovereign of the soul, directing its mind, feelings and will, Christ remains outside people's souls. Evil and passion have taken over the palace of Christ the King. These dwell there, having their orgies day and night. Christ stays outside the mind, outside the heart, outside the will. Every storey, every chamber of the divine palace, the soul, is occupied. For Christ, there is no available space. And Christ continues standing outside, knocking on the door of the soul, asking to be let in (Rev. 3:20).

Christ outside, the devil inside? What a misfortune! What a calamity!

Brothers and sisters, may God the Holy Spirit enlighten us to understand and feel our Church's invitation: "Let us all say with our *whole* soul and our *whole* mind, let us say...."

BROTHERHOOD IN CHRIST

The *Ektenes* contains six petitions. Some of these petitions, such as "For the pious and Orthodox Christians...," "For our Archbishop...," "For mercy, life, peace, health...," etc., have been explained in earlier homilies; therefore, let us interpret the three petitions heard for the first time in the Divine Liturgy. The first is: "Again, let us pray for our brothers, the priestmonks, the deacons, the monks and for the whole brotherhood in Christ." Here we will answer the question: What is the brotherhood in Christ?

Before Christ came into the world, the state of mankind was one of appalling division. There was no concept of brotherhood. The strong and powerful few took most of the fertile land by force, became masters, and the rest were subjugated to these few, having to work the land hard. These unfortunate slaves lived off the crumbs the masters threw from their tables. In Greece there were citizens and slaves; in Rome, patricians and plebians. There was division everywhere in humanity.

This division was considered natural, even by the philosophers of the ancient world. The majority of mankind, up to 90%, belonged to the slave class. They were not even considered persons, but things, with which their masters had authority to do whatever they wanted. If a master killed his slave, he was accountable to no one. A dreadful situation existed.

When Christ came to earth, preached the holy Gospel, and established His Church, this terrible situation changed. Christ changed the world and created a new society incredibly different from the one that existed. Christ God, the King of Heaven and Earth, alone Lord and Sovereign of the natural and spiritual universe, walked on the face of the earth and embraced the lowliest and despised. He called them brothers and sisters, and said: "Whoever hears my teaching and does the will of the heavenly Father, he is my brother and my sister" (Matt. 12:50).

The word "brother" refers to one born of the same mother. But, according to the preaching of the Gospel, the word also has a spiritual meaning: those who are born of the same Mother, the Church, are brothers. She is the spiritual Mother of the faithful. The Baptismal Font is this Mother's womb, and the children who come out of the Baptismal Font (which is the same for everybody) become brothers. They are spiritually connected with Christ and His holy Church. Their names are registered in the books of the Church, and they receive, to use a modern expression, *Christian citizenship*. They therefore belong to the Christian brotherhood, the big family of Christ.

Worldly distinctions are left outside the Church. There should be no discrimination in the Church. All are brothers, and the person who holds a position of high authority in the secular state, if he is Christian, should not boast or be haughty, but should be humble, holding even the poor and lowly Christian as his brother. It is possible for this lowly person to have more spiritual value before God than an official in public office.

Christians are brothers and sisters to each other, and, as brothers, sit and eat at the same Table and are nourished with the precious Body and Blood of Christ. The same blood runs in their veins – the Blood of Christ, which is transfused mystically through Holy Communion.

Therefore, everyone who is baptized, attends church, and participates in the holy Mysteries, makes up the brotherhood of "Christ-everyone" – from the white-haired old man to the infant – and it is for this brotherhood in Christ that the priest is inviting us to pray.

This brotherhood, however, should not be confined within the walls of the church. We are brothers in church, but we are also brothers outside of church. Brothers, true brothers, have everything in common, and do not quarrel, saying: "This is mine and this is yours". Christians, true Christians, who are deeply affected by the preaching of the Gospel, who feel they are members of one and the same family, find an easy way to solve economic problems, and live with love under the blessing of the Lord. If they want, they can establish a truly Christian society and brotherhood, which will be a contemporary example of the first Christian society. Please open and study the fourth chapter of the Acts of the Apostles, verse 32, and you will see a miracle, a social miracle, that the Christians of Jerusalem carried out.

Brotherhood! It was one of the three words which symbolized the French Revolution. Unfortunately, those beautiful symbols remained and still remain unrealized today, not because God does not want brotherhood, but because man does not want it. Man, with his selfishness, his self-interest, greed and rapacious plans, is the great obtacle, the first enemy, who will not allow the idea of brotherhood to be realized. For this to happen, a revolution must take place, a revolution which differs from other revolutions in that it is an internal one, a revolution of the heart. If the heart will not be redeemed, cleansed of its passions, it is impossible to create and preserve a society based on the first Christian community.

Brotherhood is needed, but it must be a brotherhood in Christ. And this "in Christ" carries great importance: without Christ, without love, even if a system of government is founded which externally resembles brotherhood, promising equal distribution of goods on the earth, this system will not have a firm foundation. It will be tossed and buffeted on the wild waves of human selfishness, and will fall into ruin.

A true society can be established only with the love which Christ taught, with a love which embraces all the people of the earth. The way things look today, we are far from this ideal of a true society. However, where there are three or four people who believe in Christ, and let their lives be guided by the Gospel, in this small group the true image of Christian brotherhood appears. And whatever these few people do in establishing brotherhood, all of humanity might do. For such a universal brotherhood, let us keep praying.

THOSE WHO LEFT . . .

Beloved in Christ, another petition in the *Ektenes* says, "Again let us pray for the blessed and ever to be remembered founders of this holy church, and for our Orthodox fathers and brethren who have gone before us, and here or elsewhere have been laid to pious rest."

With this petition, the priest exhorts the congregation to pray for all those who have lived and died in the faith. It is a petition for the dead, one that is repeated at the end of the Divine Liturgy, when at last the precious Body and Blood of our Lord Jesus Christ is on the Holy Table.

Let us consider this holy command of the Church and think of our beloved dead.

The life we live on earth, my friends, is not forever. It lasts for 70, 80, or 90 years, and rarely over 100 years.

What is human life like? Imagine a train that runs continuously, and every so often stops at a station, lets out passengers, and continues on its route. The train has one hundred stops, as many years as a man's life. When the train starts out, it is full of passengers. These are people born in the same year. Not all of them arrive at the last station. Some of them die in infancy or childhood. Death, like a conductor, will sound and call them to get off at the nearest stations, 1 to 15. And death, continuously calling, will summon others of young age, at stations which have numbers from 20 to 30. And this train goes on, letting others off at more distant stations, 40, 50 . . .. The longer the train goes, the fewer are its passengers. At the last station there are but a couple people. They are filled with sadness when they realize how many started out with them. But death will call even these few and they will be forced to leave this train called human life. Not one of them born in the same year will remain. Yet again, the train will be filled with others, and again emptied,over and over again. This filling and emptying will occur as long as human beings exist on earth.

People leave everyday! Many of them are beloved: father, mother, wife, children, relatives and friends, teachers and professors, priests and people, who worked and labored for the natural and spiritual welfare of the land. They leave, and we who are left grieve for them and our eyes are filled with tears. Some of us who left our villages when we were young can remember returning to visit after many years, being older and more mature, and going to church on Sunday. What memories! The church attendance brought to mind dear ones no longer in this life. The father of this one or the mother of that one used to stand in that spot in the church; further on, at the Analogion, the pious cantor, who used to chant and bring you to contrition with his touching voice. At the Altar you seem to see the uneducated but pious village priest of blessed memory coming out of the Beautiful Gate with his few but vivid words about the Gospel.

One visit to the parish church on a Sunday makes us remember our beloved departed. A warm prayer for the repose of their souls should be heard from the bottoms of our hearts: "Again let us pray for the blessed and ever to be remembered...."

Materialists, unbelievers, and atheists say that we completely vanish when we die. To this our Christian faith responds, "No!" The soul, which is the main part of us, being spiritual and immaterial, knows no annihilation. Death cannot touch it. It is immortal. It resides in the body, but lives on outside it; and it will live again in a new body, one liberated from death and corruption.

The body we now have holds the germ of death, death as a result of the sin of the first man. After death (the separation of the soul and body), the body disintegrates, but it is not completely destroyed. It dissolves into the elements from which it was made. These physical elements, spread by nature, will one day be reunited by the command of God Omnipotent and compose new bodies, incorrupt, untouched by death — bodies which will be greatly different from the ones we have now, ethereal bodies to clothe our souls. God's plan for the resurrection of the dead is wonderful. Those of you who want a witness for it should open your Old Testament to the 37th chapter of Ezekiel. The dead will be resurrected.

In the Gospel, we read about the resurrection of Lazarus (John 12). Please take note of one detail: when Lazarus became very ill, Christ was far away, and it was impossible in that day to know by any human means how His friend's illness was developing. But as God, He knew the time Lazarus died, and told His disciples. He did not, however, say he "died," but that he had "fallen asleep" (John 11:11) — that is his body — and that He was going to awaken him. He woke Lazarus from death, and in the same way, on the terrible day of Judgment, He will awaken the bodies of all the dead from the sleep of death.

The Apostle Paul also calls death "sleep." Writing to the Thessalonians, Paul admonishes them not to cry inconsolably when someone dies, as do those who have no hope. The dead are called "those who sleep," people who went to sleep in their graves and are the "Blessed fallen asleep" (I Th 4:13-17). St. Cosmas Aitolos, who lived about 200 years ago and preached in many places, used to say that sleep is a short death, death a long sleep, and Christ, Who raised the dead, will also awaken us from the sleep of death. "Sleep" here has reference to the body, not to the soul.

Yes, the bodies of the dead will be resurrected! The Christians of the first centuries believed this truth, and so on their tombstones they never wrote the words "he died," but rather "he has fallen asleep." The places where they buried their dead were called "cemeteries" (Gr. *koimeteria,* sleeping places), and prayers for them were called "petitions for those fallen asleep." Unfortunately, this faith has completely disappeared from the hearts of Christians today, and on the stones and crossed above their graves, the word "died" is carved, and rarely "fallen asleep."

CULTIVATION IS NEEDED

Dear reader, another petition of the *Ektenes*, the last to be explained, is this: "Again let us pray for those who bring offerings, those who do good works in this holy and most venerable church, those who toil, those who chant, and all the people here present who await from Thee great and abundant mercy."

Let us begin with an example. When I was young, I lived in one of the Cyclades Islands. The island was once a poor, rocky land. People used to raise goats and to fish, making a very poor living. There were no gardens. Fruits and vegetables were brought from elsewhere. One day, however, someone came to the island who, for years, had done gardening work. He was a man who loved to work and had a strong will. Seeing the island's need, he decided to plant a garden. He therefore chose a plot. It was full of rocks and weeds, but the man was not discouraged. He decided to overcome all odds. He set a fire and burned the weeds. He removed the stones, and where they made the land rocky, he blew them apart with dynamite. He brought in soil from other places. He dug and found water, and after a few years of long, hard work, the barren land which used to be full of thorns, snakes and goats, now was a beautiful garden. He produced a great quantity of vegetables and supplied the inhabitants of the island with food. Everyone admired the gardener and honored him as the most energetic, active, and benevolent man ever. This man has since fallen asleep, but his memory remains in the hearts of the islanders. His garden proclaims his love of work.

But, you may ask: "Why are you giving this example?" Because our society, in a way, is like a piece of land full of rocks and weeds. The rocks and weeds are the many evils, bad habits, and passions that do not allow the good seed of the Gospel to germinate. If society stays this way, nothing good will come of it. But this society, which seems so wild and prone to despair, can be changed. It can expel the evils and bad habits which have been nesting for years and years, and it can become a beautiful spiritual garden. For a society to change and become a community of prudent, temperate, just, and virtuous people, to become a Christian society, cultivation is needed. People must be found who love to work, like the gardener of the Cyclades. And, as that man labored, so also should people who desire the moral and religious cultivation of a society. An uncultivated and wild land does not easily become an orchard or vineyard.

Do you want another example? Let us look at a continent! Before its discovery, America was a wild land, full of jungles and huge fruitless trees, with swamps, marshes, nests of snakes and wild animals. The first immigrants from Europe arrived and began cultivating the untilled soil; and in a few years, this same soil began to produce fruit. With the endurance of new generations, in a period of 200 years, this land became exceptionally fruitful. It not only feeds and supports its own inhabitants, but also the people of other countries. Thanks to the hard work of its people, not a small stretch of land like the Cyclades, but a huge country, became the richest continent in the world.

But why go so far? We have the same example in our own country. What was Greece fifty years ago? It was a poor country, uncultivated and undeveloped for the most part. But our refugee brothers came from Asia Minor (namely the Microasians, Pontians and Thracians), and the population increased. And because all of Greece's children loved to work, young and old, the Greek land became fertile and this poor country became self-sufficient in necessary products.

What love of work can do! What "cultivation of the earth" can accomplish! Roses shoot up from rocks. Swampy places become plains. Wild jungles become productive, and where foxes and wolves once lived, there are now villages and settlements.

Even though our land is cultivated and makes economic and material progress, it is far behind in other kinds of cultivation, namely, the cultivation of the soul; not only the cultivation of the mind, which often turns out unbelieving scientists and atheists, but more importantly, the cultivation of the heart, of will and feeling, which makes people noble and honest in character. This spiritual cultivation takes place mainly in the Church of Christ, and the cultivators are the deacons, presbyters and bishops. When we have such cultivators, full of zeal, love of work, and self-denial, society is cleansed of devastating passions and evil; it is refined, elevated, and it brings forth fruit. The spiritually uncultivated land becomes a garden of Christ. Christ is the Arch-gardener, and the pious clergy are its lesser gardeners, and the co-workers are all those who assist the clergy for greater spiritual productivity. These co-workers with the priesthood are the trustees, cantors, custodians, doorkeepers, the faithful men and women who offer their services for the missionary work of the Church.

But are there such kind spiritual cultivators in the Greek Orthodox Church today? Unfortunately, the answer is not a pleasant one. Our Church once produced great Fathers and Teachers, and spiritually cultivated not only Her own people, but even neighboring nations. Today, however, our Church is going through a deep crisis. In many cases, our people are not cultivated at all, or if they are cultivated, they are not cultivated as much as they should be, or in the way they should be. The plowshare of the evangelical plow must be plunged deep into the souls of our people. Spiritual tractors must go to work. The rocks must be cleared away. But where are the spiritual workers? Cultivating the land is thought to be an important enterprise, and young people by the thousands are studying agriculture. But where are the young people to study in theological schools and seminaries? There are only a few, and even those numbers are dwindling, and many lose their zeal because of the present bad administration of the Church.

Dear brothers! You who care for the Church, upon hearing this petition, pray to God to send spiritual workers to cultivate extensively the hearts of men, and once again make our country a chosen garden of God.

THE CATECHUMENS

We spoke in a previous homily, dear friends, about holy preaching. Now in these final chapters on the Divine Liturgy, we will talk about the catechumens: what a catechumen is, and if catechumens exist in the Church today.

As we said before, after Pentecost, the Apostles, who had received the Holy Spirit and were furnished with divine power, went about preaching. The world was ignorant of the true God at this time. Idolatry prevailed everywhere. There were idols everywhere. There were diviners and idolatrous priests everywhere. Passion and evil had been rooted in society for centuries. Fulfilling the command of Christ, the Apostles preached in this world. They walked in the footsteps of Christ. Just as He planted the word of God in the hearts of thousands of people, so also the Apostles, like sowers, laid the seed of Divine teaching of Christ everywhere. You remember the parable of the sower (Matt. 13:3:23). The seeds which the sower planted in the ground did not all fare the same way. Three-quarters of all his seeds were lost, because they were not planted in suitable soil. They did not grow. Only a quarter of all the seeds, those that fell on good soil, produced fruit.

It was the same way with the word of God which the Apostles sowed. It did not have the same effect everywhere. There were cities in which the seed could not bear as much fruit as was wanted. Opposition was terrible. But the remarkable thing is that even in these cities which did not accept the preaching of the Gospel, there were still souls who heard and believed in Christ. These few became the nuclei of the first churches, the yeast which fell in the pagan world and would later contribute to the fundamental transformation.

Patience and persistence were needed to preach. The Church did not give up if She failed the first time. She continued preaching, and if She did not succeed the first time, She did the next. Ancient Athens is an example. Its entire population worshipped idols. It was full of idols. To this city came no ordinary preacher of the Gospel, but a renowned one, a favorite among the Apostles, Paul. The Athenians, influenced as they were by the philosophic concepts of the time, reacted. Few believed. These few were the Church. Did they remain only a small number? Certainly not! Little by little, they multiplied, and there came to be more Christians than idolaters. And after much hard work through the centuries, the entire city became Christian, and not one idolater remained in this once pagan capital.

The first Christians considered it their sacred duty to convert others to the Christian Faith. Through their simple preaching and, for the most part, through their holy way of life, they attracted idol-worshippers. And when the idolaters expressed their desire to become Christians, the Christians would bring them to the bishop. The bishop did not baptize them immediately, but he or designated priests undertood their instruction (catechism), teaching them what they ought to believe and do as Christians. This instruction usually lasted three years.

The ancient Church was in no rush to get members in a careless way just to increase its numbers, but was interested in having active members, true Christians, who had knowledge of their sacred mission. Quality, not quantity, was of more interest to the ancient Church. St. John Chrysostom used to say it was prefereable to have a few real Christians than a multitude of nominal ones who live more as idolaters than as Christians.

The catechumens were permitted to attend Church, to stand in a designated place, and attend a part of the Divine Liturgy, but not all of it. They stayed in Church, prayed with others, listened to the readings and preaching; and after the deacon said the *Ektenes* and other special petitions for the catechumens, he called them to leave the church. Only when they had all left would the Divine Liturgy continue. And because only the faithful attended it, it was called the *Liturgy of the Faithful*.

In the ancient Church, not only the catechumens were obliged to leave, but others as well: those who were baptized and registered in the books of the Church as faithful, but after baptism had not watched their way of life and had fallen into certain sins, which became known to the community and scandalized the people. Fornicators, adulterers, thieves, unjust and greedy people, gossips, blasphemers, those who denied the faith, criminals, and murderers, had no place in the church. Those who sincerely repented were later allowed to stand with the catechumens in church to attend the Divine Liturgy until the preaching was done, when they were obliged to leave.

The Church in the time of Her glory was a vigilant guardian of the Faith, and of morals. She was gentle and compassionate to those who sincerely repented, but severe to those who committed heinous sins and did not show sincere and appropriate repentence. Among these were individuals of high estate, whom the whole world held in awe and fear. She closed out generals, kings and emperors, and would only allow them entry to attend the Divine Liturgy if they showed true repentance, like that of David.

The ancient Church most certainly did these things. But what is our modern day Church doing? Unfortunately, She leaves Her doors open, and anyone can walk in and attend the Divine Liturgy without exception – individuals who have committed horrible sins, who have scandalized the people, who do not believe in anything the Church teaches, but speak disrespectfully and blaspheme. Many are attached to error, heresy, and anti-Christian organizations. Our Church has become like the unprotected vineyard. The fault rests with us, the bishops, who will not imitate the example of the holy Fathers and Teachers of the Church.

Let us hope that new days will come to our Church, when She will again be like She was in the ancient days of Her glory.

FOR THE CATECHUMENS

In our previous homily, we spoke about the catechumens, namely, those who were not yet Christians, but had belonged to other religions and then expressed a desire to espouse the Christian Faith. The Church did not receive them immediately by baptism. She had them attend lessons about the Christian faith, and after making sure their desire was sincere and their decision to follow Christ was steadfast, they were received by baptism.

The ancient Church held catechism to be of great importance. She was interested more in quality than in quantity. A few faithful, dedicated to Christ, were worth much more than hundreds and thousands of people called Christians who did not lead a Christian life. Just as it is impossible to keep an army in fighting condition with soldiers who were never properly trained, so too the living and free Church the Militant, which is conquering and triumphing, cannot exist if all those who want to be Christians are not first instructed in the sacred weapons of the Faith. Untrained Christians are worthless, and nothing noble and important can ever be expected from them. Because the ancient Church used to instruct Her members systematically before baptism, many heroes of the Faith, confessors and martyrs, came out of these ranks of catechumens.

Those who were in their period of instruction (catechism), as we have said, were able to be in church during the Divine Liturgy up to the reading of the Holy Gospel. This part of the Liturgy which the catechumens attended was called the *Liturgy of the Catechumens*. And before the catechumens left, the church would pray for them.

The deacon says, "Let the faithful for the catechumens pray to the Lord." And what are those things the faithful are called on to pray? The petition itself tells us:

"That the Lord show them mercy; instruct them in the word of the truth; reveal to them the Gospel of righteousness; unite them with His holy catholic and apostolic Church."

As you can see, in this petition the faithful are asking the Lord to have mercy on the catechumens; next, to instruct them in the word of truth; then to reveal to them the Gospel of righteousness; and last, to unite them to His holy catholic and apostolic Church.

These four petitions are very important. They show the Church's great interest in the catechumens. Because catechumens still exist in the Church today, although the instruction appears in a different form, we in the contemporary Church ought to show the same interest in these ancient petitions. Let us say it: if there were an on-the-spot examination of today's Christians, it would show that the majority of Christians are unenlightened in the great topics of the Faith, and should be enrolled in the ranks of catechumens. Alas! Although they are baptized, they should become catechumens – soldiers that have to return to boot camp for training! For many Christians, this would mean starting with the ABC's of the Faith.

But let us examine the petitions for the catechumens.

The first thing we ask for is that God have mercy on them. The mercy of God is called God's love for mankind – a love which is expressed in a number of blessings. We live in the sea of God's mercy. If God's mercy subsided, we would not live one moment more. All life depends on God's mercy. Do you doubt this? Think for a moment. The sun, the rivers and lakes, the seas, the trees, the air we breathe – all these are everything we need to live. They are not our own; they are the mercies of God, Who, as Holy Scripture says, "maketh the sun shine on bad and good people alike, and giveth rain to those who do right and those who do wrong" (Matt. 5:45).

These things are the material blessings which God gives to all people. The one who blasphemes Him day and night does not stop getting these gifts of God's love. The wind does not stop blowing for him, and the sun still sends its rays to light and warm him.

Besides material blessings, however, there is another gift, incomparably superior to all the rest. This blessing is faith, faith in our Lord Jesus Christ. It is God's gift, which He gives not to everyone, but to those who wish to believe and live according to His will. O faith! What could we do with all the riches and treasures of the world if we could not believe in Christ? Lord, give us Thy mercy, give us faith, because this is Thy most important blessing.

The other three petitions are related to the first. When a person is blessed by God with the gift of faith, the ears of his soul open to hear Divine teaching, the lessons of sacred catechism, with joy and delight. The eyes of the soul open to see the great light, the Gospel. All these spiritual gifts have their source in God. The Lord enlightens, teaches and instructs, the Lord reveals mysteries, inspires love and harmony, and leads us to wonderful unity. Every effort to return sinners to repentance will fail, unless the Lord sends His mercy into the soul. Without His help, we cannot succeed in anything spiritual or holy.

That is why the petitions for the catechumens end with the words: "Succor, save, comfort and protect them, O God, by Thy grace." The prayer which the priest sends up silently is also similar to this.

In the next homily, we will continue to speak about the catechumens. As we said before, we consider instruction more necessary in our modern Church than it ever was in the ancient Church.

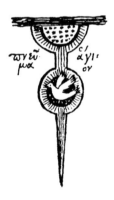

INFANT BAPTISM?

Beloved, despite all we have said in previous sermons about the catechumens, we still have not exhausted the subject. For this reason, this sermon will also involve the same topic, which we consider to be one of the most important of our Church. Our Church's situation would be quite different if instruction were given today as it was given during the first centuries of the Christian Church.

Accordingly, let us see in more detail how instruction used to be given in the ancient Church, the Church of the first centuries of Christianity.

As we have said before, the Christians of that period were few in number, compared with the pagans. However, these few Christians constituted the light and salt of the world. Their presence was noticeable. Preaching, miracles, and, most of all, the holy life which the faithful lived both as individuals and as families, attracted others to the faith. It was a time when the Church did not lose, but rather gained, souls. When a pagan was attracted by the greatness of the Christian faith and life, and revealed his desire to be baptized and become a Christian, a Christian who knew him would undertake the task of helping him. He would lead the pagan to the bishop, who would listen to the person who wished to become a Christian. He would find out whether the pagan had a sincere desire to become a Christian, whether he had decided to abandon the pagan life with all of its abominations. And if the bishop was convinced of his sincerity, he would order that his name be recorded on a special list, the list of the catechumens.

From that day on, the catechumen would attend, along with other catechumens, certain lessons. These lessons were offered by both clergymen and laymen who were recognized for their learning, and especially for their holy way of living. Catechism was not an easy thing at that time. For pagan fanatics, who followed the movements of Christians, would attack them with great ferocity whenever the place where Christians gathered the catechumens for instruction was discovered. And there were cases in which the cruel persecutors would set fires and burn the catechumens who were gathered in catacombs or caves. These catechumens were baptized with the baptism of martyrdom before they could be baptized with the sanctified water of Holy Baptism.

When the catechumens had been taught everything that they were supposed to learn, their teachers would lead them back to the bishop, and the bishop would recommend that they change their pagan names and adopt Christian ones, names to remind them of holy persons or of virtues (e.g. Agapios, from *agape*, "Love;" Elpidios, from *elpis*, "hope;" Irenaios, from *eirene*, "peace...."). As you see, the Early Church attached great importance to a person's name. Yet certain people insist on giving their children names which have nothing to do with the glorious history of Christianity, or even the names of atheists and unbelievers who waged war and still wage war against Christianity. The names of Christians must be reminders of faith and virtue.

When the pagan names had been replaced with Christian ones, the catechumens were prepared for baptism. Before baptism was performed, they were again taught lessons, lessons which were higher than the previous ones. These lessons were usually taught during Lent, the period of fasting before Easter. And on Holy Saturday (the day before Easter), which was the eve of the baptism of the catechumens, all who were to be baptized on the next day were led once more to the bishop. The bishop taught them a last lesson. At this last lesson, he used very moving words. He would tell them the end of their catechism had arrived, and that on the next day, when they would be baptized, they would leave forever the kingdom of darkness, the kingdom of satan. He would tell them that they would have to hate the devil and that they would have to love Christ with a fervent heart. He would tell them that they would have to be prepared to honor the name of "Christian" not only with good words and holy deeds, but also with their blood. In that way, they would be worthy to stand before the judgment-seat of the Divine Judge on the fearsome Day of Judgment, and to hear the words: "Come, ye blessed of My Father, inherit the Kingdom prepared for you since the foundation of the world" (Matt. 35:34).

The following day, Easter, was the brightest day in the lives of the catechumens. On this day, they would confess their faith before all of the Christians, and would be baptized and registered among the faithful in the registry books of the Church.

In this manner were catechism and baptism conducted in the Church of the first Christians.

Unfortunately, however, this system of instruction, which brought forth so many wondrous fruits and revealed the Church as vibrant and free, victorious against this world, became enfeebled with passage of time, and the day came when it was abolished completely. After St. Constantine the Great, when the new religion won out, many came forth to become Christians not because they believed in Christ, but rather because they wished to belong to the religion which prevailed as the religion of the State. These people were gathered together in rivers and lakes and were baptized by the thousands, without having been instructed, simply because they said that they wanted to become Christians. They would become Christians in name, but besides that, nothing would change in their lives. Such mass baptism occurred among the Slavs.

Moreover, the custom which prevailed in the Orthodox Church, the custom of baptizing people as babies, which is called "infant baptism" (*nepiobaptismos*), led to the complete abolition of instruction before baptism. Thus, there are only a few parents who instruct their children in the faith. Most parents are completely indifferent about the Christian upbringing of their children. In fact, there are not a few unbelieving and atheistic parents who mock the sacrament of baptism. My humble opinion is that the children of these people, who have cut off all substantial contact with the Church, should not be baptized as infants, but should rather be allowed to grow up and to freely make a decision regarding their religious beliefs.

I think that the time has come when the church is compelled, by these circumstances, to return to the system of the Early Church, to the days of the catacombs. Our motto is: "We seek a free and vibrant Church."

SUMMARY

My dear Christians, we have come to the end of the first part of the Divine Liturgy, which has been called the *Liturgy of the Catechumens*. We have studied about sixty sermons, attempting to explain in everyday language what is said and done in the first part of the Divine Liturgy. Now that we have come to the end, we glorify God, who allowed us to speak about the Liturgy and about the boundless richness of meaning which the text of the Liturgy contains. We have offered some of our lessons as paltry coins taken from the treasury of Orthodox teaching. There are texts which wise and inspired teachers of our Church wrote, and in them, anyone who desires can find something deeper and more lofty than these.

The Divine Liturgy is like a river, which continuously moves its clear, crystal waters. Whoever desires can bring his pitcher and take as much water as it can hold. A small pitcher will hold little water, a large one will hold much. The benefit a person draws from the inexhaustible river of the Divine Liturgy will be according to the faith and spiritual state he or she has while in church. There are some unfortunate people in our country who, even though they are thirsty, do not go to this river. They do not attend Church, but go to dirty waters, to the swampwater of atheistic, faithless teachings and there these wreteched people try to quench their thirst. The Church invites us: "You people of the 20th Century!

Come, drink the water of this endless fountain, the Divine Liturgy!" How few listen to this voice, and how fewer run like deer to quench their thirst at the clear waters! Unfortunately, few have a thirst for Orthodox worship.

Now that we have come to the end of the actual homilies on the first part of the Divine Liturgy, let us, by way of summary, take a short look at the material we went through.

We said that the Divine Liturgy was so arranged according to meaning that it resembled a building with magnificent architecture. No matter what side you look at you will be astonished in admiration of it. There is nothing useless – everything is assembled in a divine order. Let others admire the Parthenon as an example of the art of the ancient Greeks; we Orthodox Christians have something incomparably superior to the parthenon. It is the Divine Liturgy, founded on the rock of Golgotha.

The magnificent gateway whereby we enter the Divine Liturgy is: "Blessed is the Kingdom of the Father and of the Son and of the Holy Spirit..." Every Believer should experience a shivering emotion upon hearing this exclamation of the priest. The Holy Trinity is the greatest of all mysteries, and was revealed to the world at the incarnation of our Lord, Jesus Christ. O Christ, we thank Thee, because Thou didst make the Father, the Son and the Holy Spirit known to us through Thine incarnation. *Trinity, one in essence and undivided*! We would be wandering in the darkness of ignorance of the true God, in idolatrous delusion, if Thou didst not descend from heaven and come to earth, and had not been baptized in the River Jordan, where the mystery of the Trinity was revealed.

The main focus of the whole Liturgy is the sacrifice which Christ offered on the Cross. Everything converges on His adored Person in undivided unity with the Father and the Holy Spirit. Things of the world which are thought beneficial, good or beautiful are only a faint image of divine greatness. St. John Chrysostom, in one of his sermons praising Christ as the center of life, says: "Christ is our fulfillment; that is, Christ is the Way, the Groom, the Root, the Food and Drink, the Life, Apostle, High Priest, Teacher, Father, Brother, and Joint Heir. He is the one who was crucified and died for us. He prays for us and is our Advocate before the heavenly Father. He is the one in Whom we live and dwell; and He dwells in us. He is our Friend, our foundation and Corner Stone, and we are His own members, His land, His edifice, His grapevine, His co-workers...."

That is why we chant: "Come, let us worship and bow unto Christ.Save us, O Son of God, who didst rise from the dead; save us who chant unto Thee: Alleluia."

Christ's Person is the focus throughout the Divine Liturgy. Christ is the spiritual Sun for humanity. The natural sun does not appear in the horizon all at once, but before rising its rays dispel the darkness little by little. Bringing the dawn by continuously moving through the sky, it reaches its zenith. It shines and makes everything bright. So also Christ in His Person appeared in the ancient world as likenesses and types, especially in the Old Testament. Finally, at His birth He rose as a great spiritual Sun, a great Light. And He has remained in His Church ever since, and does not stop sending His rays and light to everyone.

The Divine Liturgy praises and glorifies this appearance of Christ in stages. Therefore, after the long and short series of petitions which the Church sends up for the spiritual and material needs of Her Children (wherever they may be and in whatever situations they may be found), we hear in the Antiphons the voices of the Prophets of the Old Testament, particularly David, who described in the Coming, the Passion and the Resurrection of Christ, quite vividly. And after the voices of the Prophets, in the Thrice-Holy hymn we hear the angelic voices that praise the Triune God, and as we said at the beginning, reveal the Incarnation of Christ to the world. After the angelic hymn we hear the voices of Christ's Apostles in the reading of the Epistle, especially the voice of Paul, who like a golden eagle flew from East to West, preaching Christ's magnificence. And finally, we hear in the Gospel reading the voice of Christ Himself. And thus we lowly sinners and unworthy servants of God, are able to hear Christ's words. These words, if followed, would make the earth a dwelling place of Christ, a promised land, an earthly Paradise.

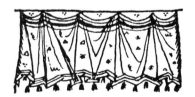

INDEX

SOME OTHER BOOKS PUBLISHED BY
THE INSTITUTE FOR BYZANTINE
AND MODERN GREEK STUDIES

ST. PHOTIOS THE GREAT

This volume by Rev. Dr. Asterios Gerostergios is devoted to St. Photios the Great (820-891), Patriarch of Constantinople, the most important spiritual and intellectual leader of the ninth century. It re-establishes the lofty Christian character of St. Photios, the purity of his life, his many-sided greatness, and the groundlessness of the charge that he was the cause of the Schism between Eastern and Western Christianity. The text is enhanced by the addition at the end of beautiful hymns, taken from the service in honor of St. Photios. Foreword by Prof. Constantine Cavarnos. 1980. 125 pp., 1 plate.
ISBN 0-914744-50-X (Cloth), 0-914744-51-8 (Paperbound)

Cloth $8.50
Paperbound $5.50

JUSTINIAN THE GREAT, THE EMPEROR AND SAINT

This volume is devoted to the Byzantine emperor Justinian the Great (527-565), one of the most important personalities of the sixth century. It is the first work that undertakes to relate the religious policy of that illustrious emperor to his religious beliefs. Written in a clear, concise and scholarly manner, it deals with the most important aspects of Justinian's personality, placing him in proper historical perspective. In this book, Justinian emerges as a very capable administrator, a wise legislator and codifier of law, a profound theologian, a remarkable author, a great defender, protector and preserver of the Orthodox Christian faith, an exemplary philanthropist, a strong supporter of monasticism, a builder of many magnifi-

cent churches, monasteries and philanthropic institutions, and a saint of the Orthodox Church. By Rev. Dr. Asterios Gerostergios. Foreword by Prof. Constantine Cavarnos. 1982. 312 pp. + 32 plates.
ISBN 0-914744-58-5 (Cloth), 0-914744-59-3 (Paperbound)
Cloth $15.95
Paperbound $11.95

ANCHORED IN GOD

The life, thought, and art of the Holy Mountain of Athos. In this fascinating and inspiring book, Dr. C. cavarnos describes the monks' daily routine of activities, including private and corporate prayer, study and work. Through questions, he elicits the views of the monks on monasticism, contemporary mankind, philosophy, solitude, fasting, prayer and other topics. An authority of Byzantine art, he gives detailed observations of superb frescoes and panel icons, pointing out the role they play in the life of the monks, and also deals with the architecture of the churches and the music that is chanted there. Out of print for many years, it was reprinted in 1975. 230 pp., 74 illus. and map.
ISBN 0-914744-30-5 (Cloth), 0-914744-31-3 (Paperbound)
Cloth $10.00
Paperbound $ 6.50

THE HOLY MOUNTAIN

A companion volume to *Anchored in God,* in three Parts. Part One is a comprehensive account of the scholars, missionaries, and saints of Athos. Part Two is similarly the first attempt to discuss the music, musicians and hymnographers of Athos from the tenth century to the present. Part Three is an account of a recent sojourn of Prof. C. Cavarnos on the Holy Mountain, bringing to light new messages and perspectives from the holy monks who dwell there. The book deals with Athonite figures of Greek and other ethnic backgrounds:

Russians, Serbs, Bulgarians, and Rumanians. 2nd edition, 1977. 172 pp. + 16 plates.
ISBN 0-914744-38-0   Paperbound $6.50

THE HELLENIC SPIRIT — BYZANTINE AND POST BYZANTINE

Twelve essays by Prof. John E. Rexine that were written over a period of twenty-five years (1955-1980) and published in various books and journals. They deal with the character of Greek thought and culture; the Church of Hagia Sophia at Constantinople; Byzantine sigillography and its significance; the Roman Bishop Liutprand and Constantinople; Mount Athos; the Church and contemporary Greek society; the poets Dionysios Solomos, Kostes Palamas, George Seferis, and Odysseus Elytis; Classical Political Theory and the United States Constitution. 1981. 136 pp.
ISBN 0-914744-52-6   Paperbound $8.50

ORTHODOX ICONOGRAPHY

Four essays dealing with the history of Orthodox iconography, the iconographic decoration of churches, the functions of icons, and the theology and aesthetics of Byzantine iconography. In addition, there are three appendixes containing authoritative early Christian texts on icons, explanations of the techniques of iconography, and a discussion of two Russian books on icons. By C. Cavarnos. 2nd printing, 1980. 76 pp. + 24 plates.
ISBN 0-914744-36-4 (Cloth), 0-914744-37-2 (Paperbound)
Cloth $8.00
Paperbound $4.50

BYZANTINE SACRED ART

Selected writings of the contemporary Greek iconographer Photios Kontoglou on the Sacred Arts according to the Tradi-

tion of Eastern Orthodox Christianity. Compiled, edited and translated from the Greek by Constantine Cavarnos. 2nd, considerably augmented, edition, 1985. 171 pp., 24 illus.
ISBN 0-914744-60-7 (Cloth), 0-914744-61-5 (Paperbound)

Cloth $10.50

Paperbound $ 7.95

BYZANTINE THOUGHT AND ART

A collection of essays by Prof. Constantine Cavarnos dealing with important but little known aspects of the classical Eastern Orthodox Tradition, the Byzantine. This work introduces the reader to the heart of Byzantine philosophical and theological thought, as well as of the arts of the Byzantine tradition, particularly iconography, hymnody, and music. 3rd printing, 1980. 139 pp., 20 illus.
ISBN 0-914744-22-4   Paperbound $4.50

MODERN ORTHODOX SAINTS

Vol., 1, ST. COSMAS AITOLOS

An account of the life, character and message of St. Cosmas Aitolos (1714-1779) – great missionary, illuminator, and martyr of Greece – together with selections from his *Teachings (Didachai)*, compiled, translated, and edited with an Introduction and Notes by C. Cavarnos. 3rd, revised and considerably enlarged, ed., 1985. 118 pp.
ISBN 0-914744-64-X (Cloth), 0-914744-65-8 (Paperbound).

Cloth $8.95

Paperbound $5.95

Vol. 2, ST. MACARIOS OF CORINTH

An account of the life, character and message of St. Macarios of Cornith (1731-1805) – Archbishop of Corinth, guardian of sacred Tradition, reviver of Orthodox mysticism *(hesychasm)*, compiler of the *Philokalia*, spiritual striver,

enlightener and guide, and trainer of martyrs – together with selections from three of his publications, compiled, translated and edited with and Introduction and Notes by C. Cavarnos. 2nd ed., 1977. 118 pp., 1 plate.
ISBN 0-914744-35-6   Paperbound $4.50

Vol. 3, ST. NICODEMOS THE HAGIORITE

An account of the life, character and teaching of St. Nicodemos the Hagiorite (1749-1809) – great theologian and teacher of the Orthodox Church, enlightener, reviver of hesychasm, moralist, canonist, hagiologist, and writer of litugical poetry – together with a comprehensive list of his publications and selections from them, translated and edited with an Introduction and Notes by C. Cavarnos. 2nd ed., 1979. 167 pp., 1 plate.
ISBN 0-914744-41-0   Cloth $8.00
                                              Paperbound $4.50

Vol. 4, ST. NIKEPHOROS OF CHIOS

An account of the life, character and message of St. Nikephoros of Chios (1750-1821) – outstanding writer of liturgical poetry and lives of saints, educator, spiritual striver, and trainer of marytrs – together with a comprehensive list of his publications, selections from them, and brief biographies of eleven neomartyrs and other Orthodox saints who are treated in his works. By C. Cavarnos. 1976. 124 pp., 1 plate.
ISBN 0-914744-32-1 (Cloth), 0-914744-33-X (Paperbound)
                                                    Cloth $8.00
                                              Paperbound $4.50

Vol. 5, ST. SERAPHIM OF SAROV

An account of the life, character and message of St. Seraphim of Sarov (1759-1833) – widely beloved mystic, healer, comforter, and spiritual guide – together with a very edifying Conversation with his disciple Nicholas Motovilov on the acquisition of the grace of the Holy Spirit, and the Saint's Spiritual Counsels. By C. Cavarnos and Mary-Barbara Zeldin. 1980. 167 pp., 1 plate.

ISBN 0-914744-47-X (Cloth), 0-914744-48-8 (Paperbound)
Cloth $9.00
Paperbound $6.00

Vol. 6, ST. ARSENIOS OF PAROS

An account of the life character, message and miracles of St. Arsenios of Paros (1800-1877) — remarkable confessor, spiritual guide, educator, ascetic, miracle-worker, and healer — together with some of his counsels. Compiled, translated and edited with an Introduction, Notes, and Bibliography by C. Cavarnos. 1978. 123 pp., 1 plate.
ISBN 0-914744-39 (Cloth), 0-914744-40-2 (Paperbound)
Cloth $8.00
Paperbound $4.50

Vol. 7, ST NECTARIOS OF AEGINA

An account of the life, character, and teaching of St. Nectarios of Aegina (1846-1920) — educator, theologian, spiritual guide, miracle-worker and healer — together with a comprehensive list of his writings, selections from them translated and edited with an extensive and illuminating Introduction and Notes by C. Cavarnos, and in addition a chapter on the miracles of the Saint and an essay on his teaching on God. 1981. 222 pp., 1 plate.
ISBN 0-914744-53-4 (Cloth), 0-914744-54-2 (Paperbound)
Cloth $10.00
Paperbound $ 7.00

Vol. 8, ST. SAVVAS THE NEW, OF KALYMNOS

Remarkable Ascetic, Confessor, Spiritual Guide, Iconographer, Miracle-Worker and Healer (1862-1947). An account of his Life, Character, Message and Miracles, together with his nine Definitions of true Monastic Conduct and photographs of many of his holy icons. By C. Cavarnos. 1985. 144 pp. 23 illus.
ISBN 0-914744-62-3 (Cloth), 0-914744-63-1 (Paperbound).
Cloth $8.95
Paperbound $5.95